# Bulrusher

Eisa Davis

A Samuel French Acting Edition

SAMUELFRENCH.COM
SAMUELFRENCH-LONDON.CO.UK

ISBN 978-0-573-66313-0
www.SamuelFrench.com
www.SamuelFrench-London.co.uk

**For Production Enquiries**

**United States and Canada**
Info@SamuelFrench.com
1-866-598-8449

**United Kingdom and Europe**
Plays@SamuelFrench-London.co.uk
020-7255-4302

Each title is subject to availability from Samuel French, depending upon country of performance. Please be aware that *BULRUSHER* may not be licensed by Samuel French in your territory. Professional and amateur producers should contact the nearest Samuel French office or licensing partner to verify availability.

## MUSIC USE NOTE



## IMPORTANT BILLING AND CREDIT REQUIREMENTS

***BULRUSHER*** was first developed in readings at New Dramatists directed by the author and later, by Seret Scott. Subsequent readings were hosted by The Cherry Lane (directed by Leah C. Gardiner), Hartford Stage (directed by Kate Whoriskey), Musefire (directed by Lorraine Robinson), and San Francisco Stage and Film (directed by Mark Routhier). Portland Center Stage workshopped the play in its JAW/West Festival, where it was directed by Valerie Curtis-Newton, with dramaturgy by Mead Hunter.

In March 2006, ***BULRUSHER*** received its world premiere at Urban Stages/Playwrights' Preview Productions in New York (Frances Hill, Artistic Director; Sonia Koslova, Managing Director; Lori Ann Laster, Program Director; Stanton Wood, Development Director). It was directed by Leah C. Gardiner.

Scenic Design and Video/Projection Design: Dustin O'Neill
Lighting Design: Sarah Sidman
Costume Design: Kimberly Ann Glennon
Sound Design: Jill BC DuBoff
Original Songs Composed by Eisa Davis
Original Score Composed and Performed by Daniel T. Denver
Additional Guitar Music by Robert Beitzel
Choreography by Jennifer Harrison Newman
Fight Choreography by Denise Hurd
Stage Management and Board Op: Jana Llynn, Leisah Swenson, Sonia Koslova, Holly M. Kirk
Assistant Stage Manager: Stephen Riscica
Assistant Director: Ronald Francis Brescio

Cast (in order of appearance)

**BULRUSHER** . . . . . . . . . . . . . . . . . . . Zabryna Guevara/Donna Duplantier
**MADAME** . . . . . . . . . . . . . . . . . . . . . . . . . . . . . . . . . . Charlotte Colavin
**LOGGER** . . . . . . . . . . . . . . . . . . . . . . . . . . . . . . . . . Guiesseppe Jones
**SCHOOLCH** . . . . . . . . . . . . . . . . . . . . . . . . Peter Bradbury/Darrill Rosen
**BOY** . . . . . . . . . . . . . . . . . . . . . . . . . . . . . . . . . . . . . . . . Robert Beitzel
**VERA** . . . . . . . . . . . . . . . . . . . . . . . . . . . . . . . . . . . . . . Tinashe Kajese

## CHARACTERS

**BULRUSHER**
**MADAME**
**LOGGER**
**SCHOOLCH**
**BOY**
**VERA**

## SETTING

Boonville, California, a small town in the Anderson Valley of Mendocino County, north of San Francisco. 1955.

The set can be realistic, suggestive, or a combination of both. Water, live guitar, and real oranges and apples are necessary.

## NOTES

Actual Boonville residents developed their own dialect of over 1300 words and phrases at the turn of the last century. The language, called Boontling, was primarily devised to discuss taboo subjects and keep outsiders out. But Boontling also functioned to document town history, create unexpected value from the strange, and satisfy the residents' overriding love of inventive talk. Boontling glossary and pronunciation guide for all local terms and the Pomo chant can be found in an appendix at the back.

The characters imagined here do not have a contemporary self-consciousness. They speak with energy and assuredness, in the rhythms of the self-made.

# ACT ONE

*(In the dark, the sound of dripping water – leaky faucet into a steel washtub. Then, a spot on* **BULRUSHER**, *entirely wet, looking up into the sky. She wears a green dress. She talks to the river, reciting her first memory.)*

**BULRUSHER.** I float in a basket toward the Pacific, hands
blue as huckleberries. This air is too sweet,
this cold water a thin, foul milk.

The woman who bore me wrapped me,
gave me to the green of the Navarro,
named me silence. She prays

this river has studied time
and will never turn back
her secret skin, the mark

that stretched into life.
Forgiveness is an insect
that may one day draw my blood.

*Catch me*, I ask the power lines,
defying the fog's quiet shroud. What is
a motherless daughter but pure will?

The river hears me and turns to molasses.
With a sharp bank through high shams,
I am born into a new language.

*(More drops falling quickly, becoming gradually slower as lights darken.)*

**MADAME.** It's gonna happen.

*(Lights up on the back parlor of a brothel.* **MADAME**, **LOGGER**, *and* **SCHOOLCH** *are in the parlor.* **MADAME** *wears a crucifix.* **SCHOOLCH** *drinks tea. It is the Fourth of July.)*

**LOGGER.** Oh you're just sayin that.

**MADAME.** I'm gonna leave here, I tell you.

**LOGGER.** Say that every summer.

**MADAME.** I mean it too.

**LOGGER.** What about your business? What about alla us?

**MADAME.** Come the Apple Show, I'll stay through the prize giving and then I'm a leave.

**LOGGER.** Not even stayin for the dance? You love the dance.

**MADAME.** It don't love me. End up hobbin by myself cause no one's got the beans to say they know me. You, you don't come and Schoolch dance too fancy. What's for me.

**LOGGER.** The music. They hire that band from Frisk to show all the Boont tunesters how it's done.

**MADAME.** You never even been to the Apple Show dance!

**LOGGER.** I heard it's nice.

**MADAME.** From me! I'm the one told you it's nice. But I can't stay out my years here, Apple Show dance or not. Feel rain comin?

**LOGGER.** Can't smell it.

**MADAME.** We'll ask Bulrusher when she get here what the river say.

**LOGGER.** I want me sweet Michelle today.

**MADAME.** Sweet Michelle is flattened with the influenzy.

**LOGGER.** Then young Elinor.

**MADAME.** She don't like you.

**LOGGER.** You don't like me with her 'cause she do like me.

**MADAME.** Elinor ain't the only one.

**LOGGER.** Well I asked for sweet Michelle. Who else you got? Cory?

**MADAME.** Her flag's out. She ain't workin today.

**LOGGER.** You call yourself a businesswoman? Never give me what I want 'cause you like to see me scramble. You like watchin the screw turn.

**MADAME.** Lucky I let you in here at all. You could have to go all the way into Ukiah for your geechin.

**LOGGER.** Who left?

**MADAME.** Well. I suppose I could let you burlap Reina.

**LOGGER.** That Mexican gal. She so set in her ways. I like to experiment, move things around some. Don't like it the same way all the time.

**MADAME.** We make the rules around here. Do it the way we like or you can go to Ukiah.

**LOGGER.** I ain't got the gas.

**MADAME.** Then take it here the way we say! And you know you only get bahl girls here. Everybody says it and we know it's true. We are the best, because we do it our own way. You don't got no stringy hair and wrinkle socks here. If you want some low quality diseased moldunes head up the pike and cool off in the oaks. But we are the softest madges you goin to find. So is it the Spanish moss or my witch's butter?

**LOGGER.** I'm tryin to enjoy myself. I'm tryin to buy me some heel scratchin. I got money and you got girls, so why you got to rout me each time?

**MADAME.** So you'll appreciate what you're gettin. Reina's up front with the rest of the girls; let me tell her you want her.

**LOGGER.** I never said I wanted her.

**MADAME.** You didn't have to. She's the quiet one, don't harp much at all. And I can see you ain't in the mood for any more talkin.

**LOGGER.** That's earth. You sure sulled me.

**MADAME.** Get your money together. You're payin up front today.

**LOGGER.** Aw girl –

**MADAME.** No more credit for you. Can't have you old dehigged jackers tryin to dish me. Makes me cankicky.

*(She exits.)*

**LOGGER.** When we gon get you a girl up there Schoolch?

*(**SCHOOLCH** is silent, but **LOGGER** converses with him anyway, judging his responses in the pauses below.)*

**LOGGER.** Let go a that teacher's English, talk a little how we talk. Harp the ling, and you can take one of these women for a ride. *(pause)* No? Well it's a shame you won't cause they all love it. *(pause)* You seein' the fireworks later? Nice out in the buzzchick field. Open view. *(pause)* You got any kids goin on to high school in the fall? I thought goin on to the upper school would be real special with all the readin of books and poetry; get you some right romantic material. Only finished middle school myself but my daddy was awful proud. He ain't had but a little education so I read the Dunbar and Wheatley to him at night.

*(**SCHOOLCH** looks quizzical.)*

**LOGGER.** Negro poets. Colored. Bookers who could write poems. *(**SCHOOLCH** is unconvinced.)* They did. A whole bunch of em. Long poems too.

*(As **MADAME** re-enters:)*

**MADAME.** Reina's in her room.

**LOGGER.** *(continuing, to **SCHOOLCH**)* I feel poetical all the time 'cause I keep they verses in my head. *(to **MADAME**)* When you gonna get Schoolch in with one of your girls? He can't be a silent seeker all his life.

**MADAME.** He won't sleep with none of them, says he's waiting for me. I just think he's scared to roll somebody he taught long division to. Time to pay up now, Lucas.

**LOGGER.** *(to **MADAME**)* You ever heard of the colored poets they had in slavery days and right after?

**MADAME.** It's 10 dollars. Don't try to shike me.

**LOGGER.** Wait now, 10 dollars? I just got a phone line put in, so I'm watchin my budget. How much a that do I get to keep?

**MADAME.** Pardon?

**LOGGER.** 10 dollars ain't what I pay. Now I spect some change.

**MADAME.** I only gave you a break way back when you were goin with me. You go with her, your same money got two mouths to feed.

**LOGGER.** You always got two mouths and both of em always wide open.

**MADAME.** Listen booker tee, ain't no call for that sorta nonch harpin. You can step right out and get your Fourth of Jeel jollies rubbin up 'gainst some tree.

**LOGGER.** Hold up, you love my nonch harpin.

**MADAME.** Only when I'm working.

**LOGGER.** Then what you doin right now?

**MADAME.** Tryin to get you to give me my 10 dollars.

**LOGGER.** Oh girl, you ain't gonna leave this town.

*(***BULRUSHER** *enters.)*

**BULRUSHER.** Evenin Schoolch. Madame. Mr Jeans.

**LOGGER.** Evenin. *(to* **MADAME***)* Take your 10 then. I need me a fresh smellin girl right now, fresh as a sprig of mint.

**MADAME.** We don't serve any other kind.

*(***LOGGER** *throws down a ten and heads up the stairs.)*

**MADAME.** Don't tell me, Schoolch, I already know, don't let no booker tee backtalk me. I know that's what you gonna say. He may not be as single-minded as you, but he's a man all the same, ain't no second class citizen. Don't tell me otherwise not on no Fourth of Jeel. What the river say today Bulrusher?

**BULRUSHER.** Clear through midday tomorrow, some mornin fog. Then a storm tomorrow evenin.

**MADAME.** Rain? Now? Well that does my garden no good. All the rows I planted are already dead from heat.

**BULRUSHER.** Your ground cover and wildflowers should take to it. This kinda rain, they'll grow right over the bald patches.

**MADAME.** That river tells you everything, don't it. Schoolch, do you realize how much money you have lost over the last eighteen years letting this girl keep her future readin skills to herself? No excuse, just plain bad business. You raised her and won't let her pay you back. And you're not even religious! You don't even go to church! This is the only place you come to with any regularity besides the schoolhouse. You come here, don't even sleep with the beautiful whores I got workin here, you just come and sit and drink tea with the madame of them all. You ain't a Christian, and you ain't a good businessman. Just a waste. And the real shame is that you never get your sexual release. It ain't nothin like tea-drinkin, I tell you.

**BULRUSHER.** Supper's in the oven, Schoolch. I done ate so you go head on, I'll see you back at the house.

(**SCHOOLCH** *looks at* **BULRUSHER**.)

**BULRUSHER.** I'm just gon sit out a while, keep the sunset in view.

(**SCHOOLCH** *exits.*)

**MADAME.** You still know how to tell people's futures?

**BULRUSHER.** I haven't for some time.

**MADAME.** I suppose everyone in this town asked you to read their bathwater by now. No fortunes left to tell.

**BULRUSHER.** I've never read your water.

**MADAME.** And that's how it'll stay.

**BULRUSHER.** Yes'm.

*(Sounds of lovemaking from upstairs.)*

**MADAME.** Alright, time to set yourself spinnin.

**BULRUSHER.** Alright then.

(**BULRUSHER** *exits and lights change. She sits, looking into the sunset.*

**BOY** *enters. He looks at* **BULRUSHER**, *then looks away. She opens a book.)*

**BOY.** Well we can't just sit here and not say nothin.

**BULRUSHER.** I'm readin.

**BOY.** No you're not, you're ignorin me.

**BULRUSHER.** Just 'cause it's the Fourth of July don't mean we gotta talk.

*(He is quiet for a moment, then flares.)*

**BOY.** I'm done with women! They don't tell you what they mean! Hide the truth of they feelins, sweeten it up with rosewater perfume, then just outta nowhere, plop. Splat. You are thrown over and no land for miles.

**BULRUSHER.** You didn't care about her no way.

**BOY.** What do you know?

**BULRUSHER.** She knew things weren't goin nowhere with you and took the words outta your mouth.

**BOY.** You know who I'm talkin about?

**BULRUSHER.** You was goin with the McGimsey girl.

**BOY.** She said somethin bout me to you?

**BULRUSHER.** You know nobody talk to me.

**BOY.** You did some a your fortune tellin on me, that's how you know?

**BULRUSHER.** I ain't never touched your water. I just used my eyes.

**BOY.** Ain't got no one to go to the fireworks with tonight. Out here talkin to you instead.

**BULRUSHER.** I told you, we ain't gotta talk. *(pause)* You ain't never talked to me before.

**BOY.** No one talk to you 'cause all you got is hard truth for people. If you was nice and not cocked darley all the time you might have you a pal.

**BULRUSHER.** Don't need no pal. Got the river.

**BOY.** Well I like bein stuck on someone, I don't care how unnatural *you* are.

**BULRUSHER.** Let's make this our first and last conversation.

*(**BOY** looks at her and smiles.)*

**BOY.** You're gonna be my new girlfriend.

*(He exits. Fireworks.*

***BULRUSHER** slams the book closed and talks to the river.)*

**BULRUSHER.** They want to know who I am.
I don't. I want to swing, swing
over the scrub pine, the hens.

They want me to lend them my eyes.
I won't. I want to snake like ice grass,
thick as a future I can't see.

But at five, I knew it all,
I read it in their bathwater;
I met them in front of the general store.

I want to swing, swing
over the scrub pine, the poppies: be a meteor,
a perfume, love the fly on my tongue.

*(Next morning.* **SCHOOLCH***'s house.)*

**BULRUSHER.** I packed a lemon for you to bring over to Madame, for tea. It's in your lunch basket.

(**SCHOOLCH** *is silent.)*

**BULRUSHER.** Heard the Gschwends say Darlin ain't gonna make it to the library to help you today. He almost lost a thumb launchin rockets in the field last night.

(**SCHOOLCH** *is silent.)*

**BULRUSHER.** Have a good day now.

(**SCHOOLCH** *picks up his books and basket, exits.*

**BULRUSHER** *plays with his water glass. Is about to put her fingers into it, then tosses the water out the window. She steps out onto the porch.*

**BOY** *is stumbling down the road, hung over, trying to keep the sun out of his face. He gets to her porch and sinks onto it to rest. He doesn't acknowledge her as she looks at him a spell. Then she walks to the pump and pumps some water into a bowl. She sets it by him on the step.*

**BOY** *splashes water onto his face, drinks some, then plays in it, slapping it like a baby.* **BULRUSHER** *sits on her chair.)*

**BOY.** Where'd you get that moshe?

**BULRUSHER.** I ain't talkin to you.

**BOY.** Your truck. Where'd you get it. Where'd you get it?

**BULRUSHER.** While back I got it.

**BOY.** I want me a truck. Always hitchin a ride to see my ma in Mendocino – I want me a truck a my own.

**BULRUSHER.** Yeah, well.

**BOY.** You got one. I can do as good as you, or better. Get me a new one. Goddamn I need a cigarette. You got a cigarette?

**BULRUSHER.** You want a cigarette?

**BOY.** Yeah.

**BULRUSHER.** They're inside the house.

**BOY.** Wait. I forgot. You my new girlfriend. I gotta be nice. I pretty please pretty face need a pretty cigarette. Please.

**BULRUSHER.** I'm getting em anyway. I'm headed into Cloverdale, pick up my oranges.

*(She goes in, but peeks out at him through the window.)*

**BOY.** *(sings)* Thorn, spine and thistle
Bramble, pennywhistle
Poisoned flowers on a vine
Sticky cockleburrs and pine
Sap that's sweet but never kind
Stuck like so much gristle
*(calls to her)* I made that one up. What kinda perfume you use?

**BULRUSHER.** *(off)* I don't.

**BOY.** There's a smell I smell when I come near ya.

*(She comes back onto porch. She has no cigarettes.)*

**BULRUSHER.** Orange rind.

**BOY.** No, sweeter.

**BULRUSHER.** Algae.

**BOY.** Come on now, say something pretty.

**BULRUSHER.** Fresh out.

**BOY.** No pretty words and no cigs? Well. Just looking at you smokes me.

**BULRUSHER.** Be seein ya.

**BOY.** Every Monday you head into Cloverdale. Pick up your oranges, sell em to the town. You must make you a lot of money. What you do with it?

**BULRUSHER.** Well I ain't givin none to you. I'll be gettin on the road.

**BOY.** The pike!

**BULRUSHER.** *Road.*

**BOY.** *Pike.* You harp the ling, maybe people would like you.

**BULRUSHER.** They buy my oranges. That's enough.

**BOY.** Schoolch won't let you talk the way we all talk, huh.

**BULRUSHER.** Don't need to.

**BOY.** You can't find out anything bout anyone in this town if you don't harp the ling. Like last night. I found out why that McGimsey girl went mossy on me – she's been bilchin Tom Soo, and his ma is Chinese! That ain't so bad, but Tom Soo? Tom Soo from *Philo*? She ain't had a taste for any tarp but boarch, so I'm glad she got inkstandy with me. Can't have no applehead ruinin my track record, sunderin my reputation. I'm a standin man.

**BULRUSHER.** I reckon.

**BOY.** I ain't afraid a talkin to you. Hey, I just splashed in this bowl a water.

**BULRUSHER.** Yeah.

**BOY.** Means my fortune's in it. You could stick your fingers in there and tell what's gon happen to me. What's my life gonna feel like? What's it gonna feel like when I touch you?

*(He reaches for her arm. She lets him touch her, then pulls away.)*

**BULRUSHER.** I only tell the weather now. Ain't read nobody's bathwater in years. After the May Bloyd incident.

**BOY.** It was you brought that on May Bloyd?

**BULRUSHER.** I just told her it was coming.

**BOY.** And you never read nobody since.

**BULRUSHER.** Sometimes I get a little taste by accident. Like in the general store and one of the twins hand me a coke got beads of water on the bottle.

**BOY.** Con-den-sa-tion is the proper name.

**BULRUSHER.** Con-des-cen-sion, I'll try to remember that.

**BOY.** So you're smart too.

**BULRUSHER.** Don't try to school the schoolteacher's girl.

**BOY.** You're so smart, you oughta tell fortunes again. Get you a booth at the Apple Show.

**BULRUSHER.** I said I ain't done it in years.

**BOY.** So you can't do it anymore.

**BULRUSHER.** I'm at the peak of my perception! I can call rain a whole week off from it coming down. I'm the best I ever been.

**BOY.** And keepin it all to yourself. People come from all over the county for the Apple Show. You could make a name with folks you never even met. You need you a manager, to publicize all your ventures. You could really make a killing.

**BULRUSHER.** For what?

**BOY.** I don't know. Why you think you got that power in the first place?

(**BULRUSHER** *starts to go.*)

**BOY.** Look, you could just tell my fortune then.

**BULRUSHER.** I ain't puttin my fingers in there. Or your bathwater.

**BOY.** What about spit? That's water, right? If you just kiss me you'll know everything there is to know.

**BULRUSHER.** One of your friends put you up to this? You messin with me just 'cause everyone thinks you're cute? Just 'cause you can?

**BOY.** Tiger lily, manzanita, you're my girlfriend. *(sings)* Oh my girl –

**BULRUSHER.** If I'm your girlfriend, prove it. Give me some-thing.

**BOY.** I ain't got much to offer a girl except my sensuality. We could take a walk through Fern Canyon, watch the salmon run –

**BULRUSHER.** It's summertime, ain't no salmon running the river.

**BOY.** There's always trout. Steelhead trout.

**BULRUSHER.** Take me somewhere where there's people and put your arm around me. Take me to the Anyhow.

**BOY.** The Anyhow Saloon? I just came from there.

**BULRUSHER.** And I'm leavin here.

(**BULRUSHER** *opens the door to her truck and slams it.)*

**BOY.** Bulrusher, be my fortune.

(**BOY** *dumps the bowl of water on his head.)*

*(sings)* Oh my girl, with the cattail curls, be mine, be mine, all mine.

*(Rain.* **BULRUSHER***'s truck is now filled with oranges. She sees a girl walking.)*

**BULRUSHER.** Hey.

**VERA.** Hey.

**BULRUSHER.** You want a lift?

**VERA.** 'Preciate it.

(**VERA** *gets into the truck with her suitcase, exhausted and soaking wet. She has covered her head in newspaper. When they see each other's faces, they are instantly struck but try to maintain their ease.)*

**BULRUSHER.** You walked all the way from Cloverdale in this storm?

**VERA.** I didn't know what else to do. Gone so long without sleep can't tell night from day, rain from dry. I come all the way from Alabama on a Jim Crow train.

**BULRUSHER.** Is that a new model?

**VERA.** Afraid not. You never heard a Jim Crow?

**BULRUSHER.** Separately, but not together. Where you going to?

**VERA.** *(removes newspaper)* Some tiny town where my uncle live.

**BULRUSHER.** Got his name? I know everybody round here.

**VERA.** Don't care what name he answer to long as he give me a place to lay my head. Conductor wouldn't give me a berth for nothing. Southern route.

**BULRUSHER.** Why not?

**VERA.** If you don't know the answer to that I am pleased to meet you.

**BULRUSHER.** We'll find him. Where in Alabama you from?

**VERA.** Birmingham. The Magic City.

**BULRUSHER.** What's there?

**VERA.** Church. Iron ore. And a Vulcan that forges everything with fire.

**BULRUSHER.** You like it there?

**VERA.** Can't stand it and I can't stand rain. Guess I'm outta luck.

**BULRUSHER.** It'll stop tomorrow morning.

**VERA.** Hope so, I gotta find me some work in a jiffy. *(realizes)* How do you know the rain'll stop?

**BULRUSHER.** The river told me.

**VERA.** Huh. *(takes this in)* My name's Vera Blass.

**BULRUSHER.** Bulrusher.

**VERA.** What's your family name.

**BULRUSHER.** Ain't got family.

**VERA.** Dead?

**BULRUSHER.** Don't know. Was born somewhere far from where I live. And my mother tried to drown me when I got born, but I guess I wasn't ready to go.

**VERA.** She changed her mind?

**BULRUSHER.** No. She sent me down the Navarro River but someone found me in the weeds. The bulrushes.

**VERA.** Like Moses.

**BULRUSHER.** No. Like me.

**VERA.** You can have *my* mother if you want – she's too concerned with being a model Negro citizen to drown anyone. *(yawns)* Forgive me, I can barely keep my eyes open. You in school?

**BULRUSHER.** Naw. But I like books. Got learnt at home.

**VERA.** What are all these oranges for?

**BULRUSHER.** Sellin.

**VERA.** So there's a street got colored merchants here? 'Cause I am howlin hungry. Ain't had a thing to eat since Texas. Would love a plate of fried fish and biscuits, cornbread and greens, ooh. *(looks into sideview mirror)* Look at my hair, oh Lord! I can't meet no one like this. Wrong as a wet cat. Why didn't you tell me?

**BULRUSHER.** You look beautiful to me.

**VERA.** Really.

**BULRUSHER.** Yeah.

*(Silence.)*

**VERA.** What kind of beauty shops in your town?

**BULRUSHER.** Mazie does hair.

**VERA.** Our kind of hair?

**BULRUSHER.** No. I do my own.

**VERA.** Looks – nice. But ain't no colored women to do it for you?

**BULRUSHER.** I'm the only one.

**VERA.** *(panicking)* What? My uncle live in a all-white town?

**BULRUSHER.** He look like you?

**VERA.** I don't know. I just know he's colored.

**BULRUSHER.** A logger lives downriver from the general store, maybe he's the one you mean.

**VERA.** He's the only Negro besides you?

**BULRUSHER.** Yeah. What's wrong? *(***VERA** *is silent.)* Well how bout some Indians? We just passed the reservation. *(***VERA** *is silent.)* If you hungry, I got an orange –

**VERA.** *(suddenly)* Let me out.

**BULRUSHER.** We're almost to Boonville.

**VERA.** Please.

**BULRUSHER.** You gotta find your uncle.

**VERA.** Let me out.

**BULRUSHER.** You can't walk back.

**VERA.** Don't tell me what I can't do.

**BULRUSHER.** Let's at least get you fed and dry.

**VERA.** I can take care of myself –

**BULRUSHER.** I can ride you back to the train station in the morning when the rain clears. Just get some rest tonight.

*(**VERA** is silent. She leans her head back on the seat and closes her eyes. They ride.)*

**BULRUSHER.** Alabama, huh. So is the dirt really red there?

**VERA.** Yeah.

*(Silence.)*

**BULRUSHER.** That must be confusing to all the honeybees. You got bees right?

**VERA.** Mm hm.

*(Silence.)*

**BULRUSHER.** 'Cause you know they like red. Huh. Red dirt. You come from a place where the dirt looks like flowers?

*(No response from **VERA**. **BULRUSHER** turns to look at her – **VERA** is asleep. **BULRUSHER** talks to the river, rapt. The storm rages.)*

**BULRUSHER.** Newspaper over
her head with the ink
just about run off.

In this dark light, I see her,
and build a pedestal
of water. She is the one,

the only one, nothing is caught
between us but my throat.
I want to say this

is a dream but it is true.
Do I know her? Is she the wet sight
of home?

*(The brothel. **MADAME**, **LOGGER**, **SCHOOLCH**.)*

**LOGGER.** *(to* **MADAME***)* I'll get Tuttle's tree up for you, but not tonight. It's a roger out there and I'm gittin back to my mink. This Michelle gives me the fiddlers! *(calls up the stairs)* Michelle, I'm comin to put in on you! Yes, I'm ready for my ricky chow!

*(***LOGGER** *heads up the stairs.)*

**MADAME.** His tree just fell on *my* property. And Tuttle has the nerve to say it is *my* responsibility to lift that log up. Isn't my tree, it's *his* tree – and I try my best to be patient – but the last time one of his trees fell in my yard, he left it layin there for three whole months! I had to plant my flower garden around it. What sort of look is that? I try to build a little civilization here, I try. But people don't have the work ethic I do, they don't understand that adherin to standards of behavior and so forth is fortifyin to the morals. And I got morals. Keep the whole of my brothel with its eye on discipline. If you don't have that, you don't have nothing divine in your life. If you can't get up regular as the sun each day, no matter what sort of cloud is cloudin ya, you ain't fit to meet God. And I'm a meet him. God will be my final savior and I will be comforted, and it won't be because I chose to give my body over to the menfolk, it won't be because I'm a businesswoman like Mary Magdalene – and Jesus *loved* her – but because I am disciplined and godlike in my approach to all things. I have nothing if not that foundation to stand upon. And so I will be revealed.

And still you judge me. What can I do to make you happy, Schoolch? How is it I can do right by God but never can do right by you? I gotta find a way to sell this place and leave this town for good. I have to see my mother's grave again. I gotta smell the grass growin there.

*(She goes to the window.)*

Bulrush here with somebody. Ooh, but it is pearlin out there.

*(**SCHOOLCH** looks as if he is getting ready to say something. **VERA** and **BULRUSHER** enter.)*

**BULRUSHER.** Evenin Schoolch, Madame.

**MADAME.** Evenin. Who's this now?

**BULRUSHER.** This Vera. She's looking for a relative of hers.

**MADAME.** Is it a man relative?

**BULRUSHER.** Uh huh.

**MADAME.** He ain't here.

**BULRUSHER.** What about the logger Mr Jeans? If he ain't the man, he might know him.

**MADAME.** *(to **VERA**)* Where you from?

**VERA.** Well, it's a little browner than here.

**MADAME.** Is it.

**VERA.** I'm from Alabam. We lost the war.

**MADAME.** We try to forget about that stuff round here. You'll get used to it.

*(Sounds of **LOGGER** and Michelle's lovemaking.)*

**MADAME.** Well you can't stay here. No offense darlin, but I don't take in no strays.

**BULRUSHER.** Schoolch, you go on home and eat – I'll make sure she's got a place to stay for the night.

**VERA.** It's alright.

**BULRUSHER.** If we can't find the logger you can have my bed.

*(**SCHOOLCH** looks at **BULRUSHER**.)*

**BULRUSHER.** It's my room. If she hasn't got a place to stay, I'm giving her my room.

*(**SCHOOLCH** looks.)*

**BULRUSHER.** I'm eighteen now Schoolch, I got majority.

*(**SCHOOLCH** exits.)*

**MADAME.** Ooh, he's upset. Well, let me call out to the logger's house then. It *is* late, you know. He most likely ain't in.

**VERA.** You don't have to call him. I'll find him on my own.

**MADAME.** It's raining child. The phone is drier and has a little less pride.

*(**VERA** goes out and sits on the porch.)*

**BULRUSHER.** *(calling to her)* Sit under the awning so you don't get wet.

**MADAME.** *(to herself)* I'll be. Another piece of cut cabbage in this town. *(to **BULRUSHER**)* Tell her to stand on the side. Don't want her affiliated with my business.

*(**MADAME** picks up the phone, pretends to dial, harried.)*

**BULRUSHER.** You got any fried fish or biscuits, cornbread or greens?

**MADAME.** There's a plate a biscuits in the kitchen. None a that other stuff. What's it for? You can't eat my food for free now.

**BULRUSHER.** It's for Vera. I'll get it.

**MADAME.** The butter and preserves are in crocks by the icebox. But don't mess up the place now, and don't get any crumbs on the counter!

*(Sounds of ceramic bumping around.)*

**MADAME.** Don't doll around in there I said! Slice a ham in the box if you want it – but put the lid back on the container, don't let it go bad. *(pretending to "end" her phone call)* Well I just rang the logger and he ain't home. You all might want to hit that hotel.

*(**BULRUSHER** comes back out with a plate for **VERA**.)*

**BULRUSHER.** *(calling to **VERA**)* I got some biscuits and ham for you Vera if you want to step in and have it at the table.

**MADAME.** No, you better wrap that gorm up and walk down to the hotel now; it's getting on into the night, wanna make sure she can get a room without any fuss. It's really not good for my business havin you two round here on a rainy night like this.

**BULRUSHER.** Vera, don't bother bout comin inside, I'm headed out there.

**MADAME.** That's right, use that common sense.

*(***LOGGER*** enters from a room upstairs. He wears only a woman's Chinese silk robe.* **BULRUSHER** *sees him and stops.)*

**LOGGER.** Heard some talk about biscuits –

**MADAME.** Oh limpin Jesus –

**LOGGER.** – and had to get right up out of that bed and see what you was hiding from me. You know geechin gets me scottied. Better give me some of those flories so I can go another round with Michelle –

**MADAME.** I just called you.

**LOGGER.** No you didn't, I didn't hear you say my name. Did you holler up to me, say, Lucas, come on down, I need you?

**BULRUSHER.** She called you on the phone. Called your house.

**LOGGER.** *(proud)* Yeah, I just got me a telephone. *(to* **MADAME***)* But you knew I was here.

**BULRUSHER.** She did, huh?

**LOGGER.** Yeah. What you want me for? *(takes a biscuit from* **BULRUSHER***)* Think I'll have this biscuit right here.

**BULRUSHER.** I got a person for you to meet. Vera! Come inside and meet a Negro.

**LOGGER.** I always say colored. That other one's too easy to mispronounce.

*(***VERA*** comes inside.)*

**BULRUSHER.** This Vera.

**MADAME.** She just came to town. I didn't want to disturb you.

**VERA.** Your name is Lucas?

**LOGGER.** Yes ma'am. Lucas Jeans.

**VERA.** I'm Ina's daughter Vera.

**LOGGER.** You Vera? *(exuberant)* Oh my goodness. Let me get my pants on. I didn't know you were coming here. Just let me splash a little water on and cleanse myself –

*(He runs upstairs.* **VERA, BULRUSHER,** *and* **MADAME** *stand in silence as he fumbles around, noisily picking up his clothes. He runs down the stairs, still dressing, and hugs* **VERA.***)*

**LOGGER.** You look like Ina round the eyes, but you shaped different. I ain't seen your mother since we was kids. She here with you?

**VERA.** No, I'm by myself.

**LOGGER.** How is she?

**VERA.** She's doin her best.

**LOGGER.** And did your daddy keep his job as a porter on the railroad?

**VERA.** He's at the steel mill now.

**LOGGER.** Well, you can only go so long bowing and scrapping for people before it breaks your manhood, that's just how it is. I wish I'd a known you were comin.

**VERA.** Didn't my mother send you a telegram?

**LOGGER.** Huh. Reckon she sent it to the sawmill. It's closed now, logging days are done. I just do odd jobs now, pickin apples and hops, herdin sheep and trainin horses. But Lord you just in, you don't need to hear all this. Let's get you some food and into a warm bed.

**VERA.** Thank you.

**LOGGER.** You already grown, land's end. Why don't I drive you back over to my region. Make a pallet for myself and you can have the ticking and boxspring, alright? You got your things, suitcase somewhere?

**VERA.** In Bulrusher's truck.

**LOGGER.** You got Vera from the station?

**BULRUSHER.** Saw her walking the road and gave her a lift.

**LOGGER.** My goodness, but that was Christian. I won't forget that, girl. Thank you for your trouble.

**BULRUSHER.** Alright. *(to* **VERA***)* Here's the food if you still want it.

**LOGGER.** *(to* **MADAME***)* Let me give you toobs for it.

**BULRUSHER.** No, I got it. *(to* **MADAME***)* Here's a quarter.

**MADAME.** Let Lucas pay. He owes me a belhoon for leavin early anyway.

**LOGGER.** You always trying to rooje me.

**MADAME.** You woulda spent at least that much on horn and chiggle if'n you kept your normal hours.

**LOGGER.** You ain't got one straw of kindness in that heart of hay do ya? I just want a tidrey of love. Just a tidrey.

*(He throws a dollar on the pool table and leaves with* **VERA**. **BULRUSHER** *walks out with them.)*

**LOGGER.** Vera, that woman ain't representative. Got a lot of honest two handed folks around here, they'll be happy to meetcha. Thanks again Bulrusher. You done a bahl thing. *(to* **VERA***)* You know I was the one told Bulrusher she was colored. She was five and didn't even know. My moshe is over here, I'll jape you home.

**VERA.** I don't know what that means.

**LOGGER.** You don't have to. Just another part of the scenery.

*(He takes her bag to his car.)*

**BULRUSHER.** If you need anything.

**VERA.** How bout an orange.

*(***BULRUSHER** *throws her one.)*

**BULRUSHER.** You gonna stay?

*(***VERA** *waves goodbye.* **BULRUSHER** *stands and watches her go in the rain. Suddenly she realizes how wet she is and smiles. Heads inside.)*

**MADAME.** Don't track mud in here, you're all wet.

**BULRUSHER.** You lied on the night of the only rain of the summer. The logger was here all the time.

**MADAME.** It's a habit Bulrusher. Think I would jenny on a customer that's got a woman asking for him? Woulda lost this madge house long ago if I was that tuddish. If you going to be a businesswoman – and I see you are enterprising with them oranges – you gotta be wise. Think on both sides of your head. Don't be afraid of anything anyone can ever say to you.

**BULRUSHER.** You woulda had us over to the hotel wasting good money on a room when he was here all the time.

**MADAME.** I woulda told him soon as you were out the door. He'd a come and found you – and didn't he? Find you? Don't judge me for what never happened.

**BULRUSHER.** I don't like to argue with Schoolch.

**MADAME.** When has he ever stayed mad with you? He can see what's goin on.

**BULRUSHER.** What.

**MADAME.** You ain't never had a – a friend. You ain't never had somebody you can see yourself in.

**BULRUSHER.** I ain't like other folks, don't need no friends. I was born to read. Born to read water.

**MADAME.** Go see Schoolch before he goes to sleep. He'll steam you but you can take it.

**BULRUSHER.** I need a beer first.

(**BULRUSHER** *exits.)*

**MADAME.** You left crumbs on my pool table.

(**BULRUSHER** *enters* **SCHOOLCH**'*s house. She is tipsy. Moves around the kitchen, soaking some beans. Distracted, she knocks over a bowl and it breaks.* **SCHOOLCH** *comes down the stairs.)*

**SCHOOLCH.** You'll replace that with your orange money.

**BULRUSHER.** Yes sir.

**SCHOOLCH.** Careless. But you eighteen! Got your majority! Telling me how old you are. I know how old you are. You are alive because of me.

**BULRUSHER.** Yes sir.

**SCHOOLCH.** You broke that on purpose to make your point?

**BULRUSHER.** No sir.

**SCHOOLCH.** Well you must want an ear settin after all the backtalk you gave me tonight. In front of a stranger at that.

**BULRUSHER.** No sir.

**SCHOOLCH.** Then what's all this somersettin for? I never expected to see you acting like this.

**BULRUSHER.** Yes sir.

**SCHOOLCH.** Like all the other children when their comb's gittin red. I thought I trained you so you'd never jump track on me.

**BULRUSHER.** I've been good. I done everything you said. I stopped readin water and tellin fortunes, did all my lessons here at home so I wouldn't be 'taminated by the children at the school. I don't harp the ling with anybody and I save up all my money steada spendin it in Cloverdale or Fort Bragg. All I do is show my 'preciation.

**SCHOOLCH.** More backtalk? My house, my rules. Break them, and you can leave here. But you won't. How many times do I have to tell you? When you were a baby, when you were just a few days old, your mama sent you down the river, sent you floating down to the brine. Wanted nothing to do with you. But you got yourself caught in some weeds and the Negro Jeans found you, brought you to the brothel tied up in his suede duster. Put you on the pool table and there you were, kicking up the smoky air. You didn't blink or cry under that hanging lamp, you just lay there kicking for your life. Madame, she ain't the kind to take pity, wasn't going to risk her business taking you in. But even if she said she wanted you, she would have had to fight me. I saw you and I felt like you had answered a question. Your eyes, the clay color of your legs, the curly hair on your head – you seemed like family, like mine. That if I had you, I'd be alright. And if you had me, you'd be alright. I knew I could protect you, I knew that you weren't supposed to be alive, that you weren't supposed to belong to me at all and that's why I needed you. That's why you fit. So there's no separating us Bulrusher, we are just like our names, bound to what we do and what's been done to us. Our names are our fates and our proper place. Don't forget that.

*(Pause.)*

**BULRUSHER.** Gotta clean this up.

*(**SCHOOLCH** starts up the stairs.)*

**BULRUSHER.** Schoolch, I was Christened at the church, right?

*(**SCHOOLCH** stops.)*

**BULRUSHER.** Did the reverend give me a name when he tapped me with the water? I got a Christian name, don't I?

*(Pause.)*

**SCHOOLCH.** Once we had another name for you, but I forget it now. You're Bulrusher to me.

*(Next morning. **LOGGER**'s house. He is tending a fire in the wood burning stove. He puts a few pieces of bread and a pot of water over the flames. **VERA** comes into the kitchen in a nightgown. It's too large; she has to pick up the hem to walk. The hem is splattered with a little mud.)*

**LOGGER.** You look like you still sleep. *(**VERA** frowns, squinting.)* "Ere sleep comes down to soothe the weary eyes." That's Dunbar. You like the morning? *(**VERA** mumbles.)* Your mother would stay in bed all day if she wasn't colored. I can't imagine what she look like now, grown and running a house. See I was always the one up and getting breakfast on. She liked to sit in the bed and play with the strings from her blanket, talk a little bout her dreams from the night before. Stare out the window like a princess waiting for some magic. My sister.

**VERA.** It's cold.

**LOGGER.** Yeah, mornings are cool here then it heats up by midday – lot different than Birmingham. I tend to ride in the mornings, but I thought I'd stay in today, hear your news. *(a brief pause, then)* I hope you brought a comb with you. I've tried not to say anything since we're just meeting but your hair looks like the burning bush.

**VERA.** Well if nobody does hair around here I don't know what I'm a do.

**LOGGER.** You don't do your own hair?

**VERA.** Mother always does it.

**LOGGER.** *(looking at her)* And it's thick too. Huh. I ain't got a pressing comb but I can plait it for you.

**VERA.** That's alright, I'll just get some rollers and smooth it down that way.

**LOGGER.** But you can't go in the store to buy rollers looking like that.

**VERA.** I'll wear a scarf.

**LOGGER.** Didn't Ina tell you always wear clean panties case you have an accident and have to get operated on in the hospital?

**VERA.** Yes.

**LOGGER.** Well why would you walk out the house with clean panties and a nappy head? That defies all reason, makes my mouth hurt to say it. I'm gonna plait your hair up before you even think about goin outside. Sit down here. And bring the comb and grease from the dresser.

*(He sits on a chair and opens his legs.* **VERA** *stands stock still.)*

**LOGGER.** Come on. I don't care if you tenderheaded, it's gotta be done.

**VERA.** You gon braid my hair? You a man. You ain't sposed to do that.

**LOGGER.** Used to do Ina's every Saturday night, with clean square parts. What am I doing explaining myself to you! Just set down.

**VERA.** You gon be careful?

**LOGGER.** No.

**VERA.** I'll just wear a scarf –

**LOGGER.** What did I just say to you? Now set!

*(***VERA*** gets comb and grease.)*

**LOGGER.** Questioning your elders, mmph. I don't know how Ina raised you but no sellin wolf tickets round here. You got you a job and your own place to stay, *then* we can put our conversation on an even plank.

*(***VERA*** is afraid to sit down.)*

**LOGGER.** I ain't tellin you again.

*(***VERA*** sits between his legs. He begins to comb and part* ***VERA****'s hair.)*

**LOGGER.** I'm gonna do it so you don't need no rollers. If you wet it and let it dry like this, when you take it out you'll have all the pincurls you need.

*(He goes to work on two french braids. Silence.)*

**VERA.** I do want to find me a job while I'm here.

**LOGGER.** Well, what can you do?

**VERA.** Type. File. Take minutes.

**LOGGER.** Nobody need none of that fingernail polish stuff round here. We'll find you something you can put your back into.

*(He combs. She looks out the window.)*

**VERA.** That Bulrusher girl said it would clear up this morning.

**LOGGER.** She's always right about the weather. You oughta pay her a visit today, thank her for her kindness.

**VERA.** Is she really the only Negro this way? I don't want to work for white people.

**LOGGER.** Used to be more of us here during boom time, but once the sawmills closed, everybody went south. Oakland, Fresno, Los Angeles.

**VERA.** But you stayed.

**LOGGER.** Keep your head still.

**VERA.** You like living with all these ofays?

**LOGGER.** It's alright. Indians are the colored folk here, what's left of em. They got it *bad.* All their land got took, they ain't allowed to go to school, and some of em can remember when they was legal slaves. So don't go lyin and sayin you're part Cherokee.

**VERA.** White folk just don't have no morals. And easy women too. Never thought I'd see a town a crackers let a buck into their bordello.

*(***LOGGER*** yanks her head to the side. She yells.)*

**LOGGER.** I know we're just getting to know each other, but I have to ask. Why you here, Vera?

**VERA.** Mother sent me.

**LOGGER.** By yourself. In the middle of the summer.

**VERA.** She needed to get me off her hands for a while.

**LOGGER.** Lean forward. You done with school?

**VERA.** Graduated Parker High. I'm going to college.

**LOGGER.** *(excited)* That's all right! *(hugs her head)* Oh Vera, I'm proud. Proud of ya.

**VERA.** I just need a job so I can save up.

**LOGGER.** College! Pretty soon you'll be a teacher yourself, huh.

**VERA.** *(with real hope)* Maybe.

**LOGGER.** Don't sell yourself short, now, you can do anything you put your mind to.

**VERA.** Mother always talks so fondly of you. Said you cut down fifty foot trees all by yourself. That white men look up to you in California.

**LOGGER.** How is Birmingham doin these days?

**VERA.** They only bomb our houses every *other* Sunday.

**LOGGER.** Yeah, I like these ofays a lot better than those. Listen Vera, you are family and you are welcome to stay. We'll find you a job, that's earth.

**VERA.** I won't be no trouble.

**LOGGER.** Love braidin hair.

*(**BULRUSHER** talks to the river.)*

**BULRUSHER.** She has tiny burns on her arm and on her ear and on her forehead near her hairline. Thin feathery scars, with crosshatching that looks like the teeth of a comb. All hot and fried and ironed – her smell begins with that – her hair, her clothes – all of her seems to have been cooked with corn oil and a strip of metal. Is it the smell of Birmingham, the steel pressing against her, burning her skin? Is that where her scars are from?
I want to dream of her.

*(**SCHOOLCH**'s porch. **BULRUSHER** is cleaning her shotgun. **VERA** enters.)*

**BULRUSHER.** Hey.

**VERA.** Hey. It stopped raining.

**BULRUSHER.** Yeah. You sleep good?

**VERA.** No. After the rain it was too quiet. Silence in my ears all night.

**BULRUSHER.** You don't like it?

**VERA.** I just never heard darkness before. Is it too early to visit?

**BULRUSHER.** No. I been up, out in the woods, catching some dinner.

**VERA.** You used that gun?

**BULRUSHER.** Mm hm. Want to see what I shot?

**VERA.** That's alright.

**BULRUSHER.** Sure? I ain't cleaned her yet –

**VERA.** It's alright. Thanks again for helping me last night. Hope I didn't get you in trouble.

**BULRUSHER.** Well, Schoolch never speaks to me otherwise so I think of it as a special occasion.

**VERA.** I don't want to step on anybody's toes. Especially when I got to find a job.

**BULRUSHER.** I never even seen anyone like you.

**VERA.** We look just the same.

**BULRUSHER.** No we don't. You're pretty, like the kind you feel inside of yourself when you go to the movies and think you're in it?

**VERA.** Yeah? You never seen another colored girl before?

**BULRUSHER.** No. I had to drink some beer just to get over you.

**VERA.** Beer? But that's only for men! You'll grow hairs on your tongue you keep that up.

**BULRUSHER.** I been doin it since I was twelve! Are there hairs?

(**BULRUSHER** *opens her mouth.)*

**VERA.** Let me see your – open wider. *(She looks.)* Looks clean, but your tongue is real long. You have to be careful.

**BULRUSHER.** But I don't like whiskey. What else am I gonna drink at the Anyhow?

**VERA.** The Anyhow?

**BULRUSHER.** Saloon.

**VERA.** They let you drink at a saloon?

**BULRUSHER.** Something wrong with that?

**VERA.** And you walk right in the front door?

**BULRUSHER.** Ain't no other door.

**VERA.** I used the front door once at Pizitz. Department store. We supposed to use the back entrance, in the alleyway, by the trash – but I strode right in the front.

**BULRUSHER.** Why are you supposed to use the back?

**VERA.** I went to buy some doughnuts and they came to throw me out. Back door, they said. My pocket got caught on the door handle when they were pushing me, and the whole front panel of my dress just came off. Came off right in this cracker's hand. And he got so red when he saw my stockings, he just walked off real fast. The bus wouldn't pick me up. Had to walk all the way home holding myself with newspaper.

(**BULRUSHER** *looks at her.*)

And it's the dark that scares me, huh?

**BULRUSHER.** You gonna stay?

**VERA.** If you'll be my friend.

**BULRUSHER.** I'll take care of you, whatever you need.

**VERA.** *(smiles)* So what do y'all do around here? For fun?

**BULRUSHER.** Drink. The Apple Show is coming up though. Big dance for that.

**VERA.** Applesauce, huh.

(**BOY** *enters.*)

**BOY.** Whoa, seein dubs. Whose sneeble are you?

(**BULRUSHER** *aims her gun at* **BOY***'s crotch.*)

**VERA.** Bulrusher!

**BULRUSHER.** Show her some manners.

**BOY.** That thing ain't even loaded, you just cleaned it.

**BULRUSHER.** She ain't nobody's sneeble. Introduce yourself proper.

*(She pokes him with the gun.)*

**BOY.** Pleased to make your acquaintance.

**VERA.** I'm Vera, pleased to meet you.

**BULRUSHER.** Say *your* name.

**BOY.** Damn Bulrusher, take that highgun offa me!

**BULRUSHER.** Say it.

**BOY.** I'm Wilkerson, *enchanté.*

**BULRUSHER.** Your whole name.

**BOY.** Streebs Wilkerson –

**BULRUSHER.** Streebs, which means strawberries –

**BOY.** Don't tell her that –

**BULRUSHER.** – 'count of the red birthmark he got on his balls.

**BOY.** You supposed to be my girlfriend, don't go spreading lies. *(to* **VERA***)* She ain't even seen my privates.

**BULRUSHER.** Don't need to, as much as you talk about em. He says I'm his girlfriend but he didn't even talk to me last night at the Anyhow.

**BOY.** We're in the early phases of love. You all kin?

| **BULRUSHER.** | **VERA.** |
| --- | --- |
| She kin to Mr Jeans. | I'm kin to Mr Jeans. |

**VERA.** From Birmingham.

**BOY.** My great granddad died over you, tryin to keep the Union together.

**VERA.** You think us colored folk are worth it?

**BOY.** What?

**VERA.** Death.

**BOY.** Haven't really sized up the race as a whole.

**BULRUSHER.** Yeah. We are.

**BOY.** You ain't colored, you a bulrusher and a fortune teller. And you my girlfriend.

**BULRUSHER.** Just 'cause you say something don't make it true. Get off my porch 'fore I load up this gun and use it.

**BOY.** Aw, manzanita –

**BULRUSHER.** Off.

**BOY.** I'll stack your oranges for you nice and tight.

**BULRUSHER.** What did I say.

**BOY.** Don't be so teet lipped. Leavin me all dove cooey. I just wanna see your golden eagles.

(**BULRUSHER** *chases him off. As he exits, he yells:)*

You can't get rid of me, doolsey boo, no no! I'm gonna geech you!

**VERA.** What's a sneeble?

**BULRUSHER.** Like a snowball. It's the funny way to say Negro.

**VERA.** And you'd point a gun at a white man for that?

**BULRUSHER.** He's a boy. I won't have him treat you wrong.

**VERA.** Fred – my boyfriend at home – he'd never do what you just did. He fears the Lord God. He did steal me a pickle dipped in Kool-Aid powder from the store once, but that's about it. Sneebles. Why's everyone talk so funny here?

**BULRUSHER.** They're harpin the ling. Folks made it up a while ago to tell jokes and secrets, to make everything they talk about something they own. I can harp it but I don't. Made up my own way to talk instead, a way to talk to the river. I tell stories, make poetry, like I'm writing my own book. I tell things over and over so I can understand em. Hey, you really want a job?

**VERA.** Yeah. Need one bad.

**BULRUSHER.** I'm thinking of expanding my business. Summertime and all, oranges always do good, but I thought I might sell some lemons.

(**VERA** *laughs.)*

**BULRUSHER.** What? If lemons don't please you, we could try pineapples. Or bananas.

**VERA.** You want my help?

**BULRUSHER.** Sure. We could split our yield clear down the middle.

**VERA.** You sure? All I done is office work.

**BULRUSHER.** I'll teach you what you need to know. How to choose the ripe ones, how much to charge on the road versus my regulars buy crates. You're smart enough; you won't have to pay me no mind after the first day.

**VERA.** *(laughing)* Applesauce *and* lemonade. And I thought California didn't have nothing else in it but movie stars and palm trees.

**BULRUSHER.** You don't want to work with me?

**VERA.** Of course I do, I was just kidding you. It's how I say thanks.

**BULRUSHER.** I got a twang in my stomach when you walked up today. Then it spread all over. Still feels like there's turpentine under my skin. You did all that to me. Wait till I tell the river.

**VERA.** You something else.

*(The brothel porch. A month and a half later.* **LOGGER** *sings.* **BOY** *accompanies him on his guitar.)*

**LOGGER.** *(sings)* Oh she caned me with her look
She slayed me with her eye
But I had her sweet jerk once
And for it I would die
And for it I would die
And for it I would die

She turned me like a horse
She reined my wildness in
But every time she pats my rump
Oh Lord I want to sin
Oh Lord I want to sin
Oh Lord I wants to sin

**BOY.** That's an old song from the mill ain't it. Pa sang it different. You changed the words.

**LOGGER.** Naw, the song changed on *me.* I can't sing it like we used to 'cause I don't feel it that way anymore. I mean, they got electric saws now.

**BOY.** What's the electric saw got to do with a girl?

**LOGGER.** I'm saying! I mean, I came out here from Birmingham when I was about your age and that whole field in front of you was a stand of conifers. Used to ride my Appaloosa over that ridge with your pa, just take in the country. Built my own house. Not with siding, not with half logs. Tongue and grooved my own cabin all from redwood I felled myself. Now you're lucky if you see a pygmy tree.

**BOY.** Where's the girl in that?

**LOGGER.** Right! All through the valley, up and down the coast, the trees are gone and so is my youth – I have nothing left to destroy. Nothing fallin around here but apples on sheep.

**BOY.** Yeah, I'm kinda weary of doin what all everyone else do. I mean I'm not different from nobody, I'm just not always the same. Hey, I got a new song to keep me company. You wanna hear it?

**LOGGER.** Not one of them lonesome tunes now.

**BOY.** Oh I can't write those. I just missed the draft to Korea, got all my days in front of me, so I think I got a right to be happy, to sing a happy song.

**LOGGER.** Alright. Ply it for me. But soft now. I don't want to get jangled. Too pretty an evening for nothing loud.

**BOY.** It's in a new key I found, real sweet. *(He plays a chord.)* Isn't that bahl.

**LOGGER.** See what'n all you got jacker, ply your song.

**BOY.** *(sings and plays guitar)*

Twelve nights of hard liquor
Sent Rowan to his grave
He saw the lights of Galilee
And Mary just the same

And if you call for Rowan now
The road'll answer back

He's twelve nights gone to perfidy
Spread on a burlap sack

Oh save me in my nightly walk
Save me in my days
Don't want to go like Rowan Hale
I'll keep my goodly ways

Oh save me in my nightly walk
Save me in my days
Don't want to go like Rowan Hale
I'll keep my goodly ways
I'll keep my goodly ways

**LOGGER.** Huh. That's your happy song? You got kinda loud at the end there.

**BOY.** I didn't know what I was sayin for a minute and I sang with my full power to get me through.

**LOGGER.** And you made that tune up.

**BOY.** Most of it.

**LOGGER.** Clearly, you been inspired – but stop that loud singing. It sounds like you wanna hurt somebody. Don't you got a gal?

**BOY.** Yeah, I'm gettin her.

**LOGGER.** Well what you doing about it? You need to marry and set up house. That's what you oughta do since you ain't in the service or a travelin man. Need you a wife.

**BOY.** You ain't had one.

(**MADAME** *enters with glasses on, reading a letter.*)

**MADAME.** Are you comin in today or are you just tryin to hoot on me by sittin on my stoop?

**LOGGER.** If you got any vision in that pinchy face of yours, you could see I am whittlin and warblin with this yink here.

**MADAME.** Yes but I don't see either a y'all payin my loiterin fee. If you gonna porch up and tell jonnems and wess all day, fine by me but you have got to give up some rent.

**LOGGER.** "There is a heaven, for ever, day by day,
The upward longing of my soul doth tell me so.
There is a hell, I'm quite as sure; for pray,
If there were not, where would my neighbours go?"

That's some Dunbar for ya Madame, Paul Laurence. Better get you some compassion 'fore you die.

**BOY.** I was playin some songs on the guitar. You want to hear another one I wrote, Jeans?

**LOGGER.** Well, just play some chords, what all you strummed on that last one. None of them words, just the strings vibratin. That's all I want to hear.

**BOY.** Airtight.

(**BOY** *strums.*)

**LOGGER.** Madame, you ain't been honest with me.

**MADAME.** What now.

**LOGGER.** You ain't always been this hard. You used to be another kind of woman, kind got gentleness swaying out her like a breeze.

**MADAME.** I am the same woman you have always known, Lucas, I still got wind for ya.

**LOGGER.** You would hold me before; before you wouldn't let me go with the other girls.

**MADAME.** *(evasive)* There's more paperwork now, I got more things to take care of.

**LOGGER.** You put me out. You had me in your arms and then you shunted me like I had the tuberculosis.

**MADAME.** Well, I started to lose my business sense with you comin so regular – I had to draw a line just to clarify.

**LOGGER.** I ain't happy with the way my life looks. With Vera here got me thinking. I'm a 46 year-old grizz and I don't know what is ahead of me. Like this tweed here. He's comin into his manliness and he got all sorts of gals to choose from for to make a future. My future is done. All I got left is the past.

**MADAME.** You still active in your daming. You don't miss a weekend here.

**LOGGER.** And that ain't appealin to me no more. It feels like I'm just eatin the same Thanksgiving meal over and over – I get all stuffed up and nothing tastes good enough anymore to be thankful for.

**MADAME.** So that's it? Tradin in your riding crop for a chastity belt?

**LOGGER.** I just want to settle myself into somethin more wholesome. I want to feel someone. The same someone every night.

**MADAME.** Pay me and I'll hold your hand.

**LOGGER.** I don't want it that way. I want it for real. I know Schoolch has been on you for the same thing but –

**MADAME.** What you askin me, Lucas.

**LOGGER.** I don't know. You've been good to me, more than any other woman I know – I just want a real home and a quiet con*tent* in the evenings steada all this skee swillin and boisteration. I don't got a ring or nothin like that –

**MADAME.** Oh you have lost your skull fillin now.

**LOGGER.** I just want to give something over. I want to smush myself into you.

**BOY.** There's another song I got – I can play just the chords to that. Kinda gettin tired of this one –

**LOGGER.** Well pluck another song then.

**BOY.** That's what I'll do.

*(He strums another song.)*

**MADAME.** Lucas, I can't marry you.

**LOGGER.** That's just your knee jerking.

**MADAME.** Apple Show almost here. Just got this letter from someone who wants to buy this place, make me rich. How can I marry you when I'm leavin?

**LOGGER.** You didn't even think about it.

**MADAME.** I have – for longer than you want to know.

**LOGGER.** You've been wanting this?

**MADAME.** I don't run my life by what I want, Lucas. That ain't my way.

*(Lights shift to* **BULRUSHER** *and* **VERA**. **BULRUSHER** *talks to the river as* **VERA** *sings.)*

**BULRUSHER.** She is a mirror.

**VERA.** *(singing under* **BULRUSHER***'s words)* For all we know

**BULRUSHER.** A mirror. Schoolch never allowed any mirrors in the house.

**VERA.** This may only be a dream

**BULRUSHER.** I always think about touching her skin. It's just like mine only smoother.

**VERA.** We come and we go, like the ripples on a stream

**BULRUSHER.** She says that I am beautiful. She says she wants to stretch herself over me like taffy so everyone can see my sweetness. But I want to do that to her.

**VERA.** So love me tonight, tomorrow was made for some

**BULRUSHER.** I don't care about anything else.

**VERA.** Tomorrow may never come, for all we know

**BULRUSHER.** We sell fruit.

**VERA.** *(speaking to unseen customer)* They're sweet. Nickel a piece.

*(As the scene continues, they do not speak to each other, but continue to be in their own separate worlds.)*

**BULRUSHER.** I eat with her every day, pick her up from her uncle's house by Barney Flats.

**VERA.** I have never been served food by a white woman before. I sat at the table with my napkin folded in my lap and she poured milk into my glass.

**BULRUSHER.** I take her with me to Cloverdale and we buy oranges and lemons and bananas and she sings next to me in the truck. Once she put her fingers on my knee and spelled my name up my thigh.

**VERA.** Bulrusher, why don't we go to the beach? Can't you see us running along the sand and tearing off our stockings?

**BULRUSHER.** One day she kissed my cheek to say goodbye. I grabbed her hand.

**VERA.** I'm saving up my money. And I eat anything I want. Sometimes just bread with mustard.

**BULRUSHER.** She wants to go to the ocean with me but I don't like the ocean. That's where my mother wanted me to die. You're my river. I'll bring Vera to you instead.

*(The river.* **BULRUSHER** *and* **VERA** *now talk to each other.)*

**BULRUSHER.** *(to* **VERA***)* I guess I can tell everybody else's futures because I don't know my own past. I was supposed to die, but I didn't, so I think I got an open ticket to the land of could be.

**VERA.** You like reading water?

**BULRUSHER.** Only if the person want to know the future. If she don't then it's all garbled up, can't read a thing. Image gets blurry, blinds me even. *(she picks up a twig and turns it on* **VERA***)* Sometimes I wish I did water witching instead 'cause no one ever minds finding water and water never minds being found.

*(They laugh.)*

Have you ever tried wild blackberries? Here.

**VERA.** They're sour.

**BULRUSHER.** They're almost ready.

**VERA.** What about these?

**BULRUSHER.** Poison.

**VERA.** And these? They smell like being sick.

**BULRUSHER.** Just juniper berries. If you're sick, you need these eucalyptus leaves. They'll cure anything that's hurtin your chest from inside.

**VERA.** This water'll cure me!

*(***VERA** *takes off her clothes and jumps into the river in her slip.)*

**VERA.** I just want to be clean. I'm clean here, right? You can see I'm clean.

**BULRUSHER.** Yeah, I can see.

**VERA.** Then why aren't you getting in?

**BULRUSHER.** I don't know.

**VERA.** There're fish!

**BULRUSHER.** Stand in the sand.

**VERA.** It's deep.

**BULRUSHER.** There's a branch above you, hold onto that.

**VERA.** Nobody else come down here?

**BULRUSHER.** Only me. This is my secret place on the river.

**VERA.** Your river. It's your diary, your church, your everything.

**BULRUSHER.** Yeah, has been.

**VERA.** Well, your river is making me cold, so you should get in.

**BULRUSHER.** It's not cold, you're in the sun.

**VERA.** I don't want to die in here.

**BULRUSHER.** Why would you die?

**VERA.** Because it's quiet. Everything's so quiet. It makes me want to cry.

(**VERA** *laughs.*)

**BULRUSHER.** The river holds you. Anything that you are scared of, it'll hold for you. I asked the river to save me when I was a baby girl, and it held me.

**VERA.** Is that why you won't get in? You're scared your luck will run out?

**BULRUSHER.** I've just never taken anyone down to this water. I always come here alone to talk and listen and I don't know how to do that with you here too.

(**VERA** *starts to get out.*)

**BULRUSHER.** No, you stay, I just can't get in with you.

**VERA.** I'm done. I got in and I'm gettin out.

**BULRUSHER.** Stay in longer, it's only been a minute.

**VERA.** Nothing to do if you're not in with me. Can't splash, can't play – and I don't hear the river saying things like you do so I suppose I'm just a little less entertained.

**BULRUSHER.** Wait – don't get out. I'll put my feet in.

**VERA.** I'm naked as a plucked chicken in an apron! You take off your clothes too.

**BULRUSHER.** Why?

**VERA.** Because we're here together. So we're gonna do the same thing.

*(***BULRUSHER** *takes off her shoes. She takes off her shirt and then* **VERA** *pulls off her trousers for her.* **BULRUSHER** *is startled then begins to laugh. She dives in wearing her undershirt and bloomers.)*

**VERA.** You don't wear a bra?

**BULRUSHER.** What's that?

**VERA.** For to keep your chest up. They'll start draggin in the dust if you don't strap those things.

**BULRUSHER.** I didn't know you were supposed wear anything else.

**VERA.** You have been raised by wolves and none of em female.

*(***BULRUSHER** *touches one of* **VERA***'s tiny scars.)*

**BULRUSHER.** What are these scars?

**VERA.** From my mama tryin to straighten my hair with a hot comb. But I'm a country girl now. Can get my hair wet as I want. Handstand!

*(When* **VERA** *comes up,* **BULRUSHER** *touches* **VERA***'s neck.* **VERA** *holds* **BULRUSHER***'s hand to her wet neck and collarbone.)*

**VERA.** Have you ever noticed that white people smell like mayonnaise?

**BULRUSHER.** You don't want to go back to Birmingham.

**VERA.** Some days I could kill them all.

**BULRUSHER.** You're scared.

**VERA.** White folks are the ones should be scared 'cause we ain't takin what they're servin much longer. If they'd just read the Bible sometime they'd see what's coming for em.

**BULRUSHER.** Your mother misses you; she will cut her finger on the edge of a letter. But it isn't from you, it's a notice from a contest at the radio station.

**VERA.** I entered it in May.

**BULRUSHER.** You'll win a year supply of Dixie Peach Pomade and a subscription to Jet Magazine. What's all that?

*(**VERA** takes **BULRUSHER**'s hand off of her neck.)*

**BULRUSHER.** I'm sorry.

**VERA.** You didn't ask if you could do that.

**BULRUSHER.** I didn't mean to.

**VERA.** That wasn't fair. I can't see *your* future.

**BULRUSHER.** It just happened. I couldn't read if you didn't want me to. I just wanted to touch your skin – like you wanted me to.

**VERA.** So what? So my mother didn't send me here. So I came here on my own. But that isn't all you saw.

**BULRUSHER.** No.

**VERA.** Then say it. Say what I already know.

**BULRUSHER.** It doesn't matter.

**VERA.** I wanna hear you say it.

**BULRUSHER.** I said I'd take care of you, that ain't gonna change now.

**VERA.** Say it.

**BULRUSHER.** I'll start tellin fortunes again, make us some more money – you don't have to worry bout nothin.

**VERA.** You can't fix everything! Some things are just wrong and always will be.

**BULRUSHER.** Not you.

**VERA.** Yeah me.

**BULRUSHER.** So that's why you're here.

**VERA.** Don't make me explain. Just say it. Say it.

**BULRUSHER.** You're gonna have a baby. A boy.

**VERA.** A boy?

**BULRUSHER.** But I won't let you stand up to work, I'll do all the lifting. You can just sit and count the money.

**VERA.** I'm not gonna have a boy. Or a girl.

**BULRUSHER.** Yes you are. And he's gonna be as pretty as you.

**VERA.** I don't want it. All I need is the money to get rid of it.

**BULRUSHER.** He's yours. Don't say that.

**VERA.** Then you don't really want to help me.

**BULRUSHER.** Why would you want to get rid of a child?

**VERA.** You don't know where it came from.

**BULRUSHER.** But he's in you now.

**VERA.** I don't care 'cause I'll never love it.

**BULRUSHER.** You can just give him to me.

**VERA.** No! I never want to see its face! If you don't want to help me, that's fine. That's fine.

*(**VERA** gets out of the water. **BULRUSHER** follows her, quiet. )*

**VERA.** If you tell anybody –

**BULRUSHER.** I won't.

*(**BULRUSHER** turns away from **VERA**. They both put on their clothes in silence.)*

**VERA.** Bulrusher.

*(**BULRUSHER** turns toward her and **VERA** buttons **BULRUSHER**'s shirt. **VERA** kisses her.)*

**VERA.** I guess I can't hide anything from you, huh.

*(She kisses **BULRUSHER** again. **BULRUSHER** is crying. **VERA** kisses **BULRUSHER**'s tears, then her lips as the lights fade.)*

## ACT TWO

*(Same evening. The brothel.* **BOY,** **MADAME,** *and* **LOGGER** *are drunk by now and* **SCHOOLCH,** *sober, has joined them.* **BOY** *continues to play his guitar.)*

**LOGGER.** See this woman is an artisan. Don't you remember when you used to have me in your boudoir, this is years ago, boom time, and serve me some of that pecan coffee cake? Sometimes had raspberries too. 'Course you got the berries from Gowan's since everything dies in your garden, but that made sense to me. Seems if you are running a brothel proper, it should look real inviting but not feel like you could really live there. The kinda place you can't wait to get back to but so intense you can't stay? That's 'cause you are an artisan. And trained all your women good.

**MADAME.** Well I also train the men. If he's afraid of the woman in front of him, if he thinks he makes the rules, if he don't listen, he can't get nowhere with me. If I see a man got potential, I'll send him to one of the other girls, watch how he touch her. If he is the slightest bit distracted, that is his downfall. I'll tell him. You're distracted. Downfall of mankind! I'll come out and show him what he ought to do and how. Most men ain't used to that – having someone take enough of an interest to increase their skills. But I'm an artisan and on occasion a man can arouse me into my creativity.

**LOGGER.** You never had to teach me nothin.

**MADAME.** Yeah, you were probably practicing on them horses.

**LOGGER.** I'm a natural, honey, and you know it. Why? Because I know how to talk. And I know how to listen. You used to take me in, 'stead of sendin me with the other girls, 'cause with me you could empty yourself out. Tell me all kinds of stories bout yourself. And after that, I'd slip you out of your bodice and let you lay there. I could see all your moles and freckles, the streaks and scars and blushes. I wanted to turn your bright skin red, from inside. Have it run at top speed, have your heart race your own curves. You were open and draped in those smooth sheets – and I don't know if I was feelin love, but when I look back, I sure want to call it that.

**MADAME.** Huh. You hear that, Schoolch? And this is the one talkin bout marryin me. Braggin on himself steada beggin on his knees.

**BOY.** How bout we sing the Wabash Cannonball?

**LOGGER.** Ain't braggin. Tellin the truth. You want me so much it makes *my* bones ache.

**MADAME.** Ha! I don't want you! I'm sellin and I'm gone. I'm like Schoolch here – kept my feelins in the cupboard so long I don't need em. You're just like old china. Never gonna use you.

**BOY.** You know Schoolch actually taught us the Wabash Cannonball in class, stood up on his desk and looked right at us and his eyes filled up when he sang. He sang so strong, his hair moved, like he was standing on the top of a real cannonball train. And if that train was real, I figured my daddy had to be on it, that he'd left me and my ma on a machine so fast people had to sing about it.

**LOGGER.** Oh I miss your pa. You know I was there when you were born. Your pa cut your umbilical with my barlow when the midwife got ridgy. Yeah, we felled plenty pine together. How's your ma?

**BOY.** Still working at the hotel in Mendocino.

**MADAME.** When you gonna get yourself grown and start taking care of her?

**BOY.** I don't know.

*(He strums his guitar. As* **VERA** *and* **BULRUSHER** *enter:)*

**BOY.** If I had me a wife, I could do anything.

**LOGGER.** If I had me a wife.

**MADAME.** Where you two been?

**BULRUSHER.** Went swimming down on the river.

**BOY.** *(almost singing, to* **BULRUSHER***)* If I had me a wife…

**MADAME.** Well, you look distracted. And you don't need to stand that close to each other.

**LOGGER.** Like two redwood saplings. Vera here going to college, and Bulrusher got her business? They *should* stand close to each other.

**BULRUSHER.** I like standing here.

*(Pause.)*

**VERA.** I'm feeling pretty tired.

**LOGGER.** Well then we'll say good night to Madame here. And don't slip and call her Madam – 'cause she will curse you out in French.

**BULRUSHER.** I can take Vera home.

**LOGGER.** That's alright. It's on my way. So Madame, you think about what I asked you.

**MADAME.** I told you, I'm signing this place away. Settlin accounts with the girls and leavin soon as the cash is in my palm. None of those plans include you.

**LOGGER.** You know you ain't left town since that year your mother passed. Unless you got another mother you been hidin from us, you stayin put.

**BOY.** Before you go, I want to say something.

**LOGGER.** I'm sure you do.

**BOY.** It's a public announcement and it's got to be made. *(to* **BULRUSHER***)* I'm ready to put my arm around you, Bulrusher.

**LOGGER.** This a new song you wrote?

**BOY.** I'm gonna put my arm around you where the people can see. I'll take you to the Anyhow and stand by you. I'll never leave you.

**MADAME.** See what you started Lucas?

**BULRUSHER.** Why? Why you wanta stand by me?

**BOY.** I told you I'm a standin man. I've known you all my life.

**BULRUSHER.** But you ain't never talked to me till last month.

**BOY.** I was shy.

**BULRUSHER.** You didn't want to put your arm around me because I'm colored.

**BOY.** What? No. I just thought you were a witch! Everybody says you don't have no ma, you just got spit out the river by the devil's tongue.

**BULRUSHER.** And who said that about me? White people.

**LOGGER.** Listen now, you can't say that Bulrusher. You know the reason no one talks to you is 'cause you ain't got no family. Whoever gave birth to you didn't care nothing for you, but this white gentleman Schoolch has cared and cared hard.

**BULRUSHER.** So this Boy wants to be like Schoolch, wants to save me?

**BOY.** I figure if he lets me be with you, if you let a bloocher like me into your pasture, that's proof I can do anything in this world.

**BULRUSHER.** You don't even know what you want to do.

**BOY.** I want to choose you. You pulled a gun on me. It wasn't loaded, but it was passionate. No girl's ever done that to me before.

**BULRUSHER.** I'll do it again.

**BOY.** See? Some people don't need reasons – they just know. They just have hearts and certainty. That's what's happening here. And it may seem strange to you because you ain't inside my heart and feeling it pound, but some things are just for sure. You are that. You are my for sure.

**BULRUSHER.** What are you talking about?

**BOY.** I'm choosing you! The witch! Why can't you just be chosen? Sometimes that's all people need. To be chosen, to be the only one. I'm a do that for you. You don't have to do it for me if you don't want to, but I'll make it easy for you to change your mind.

**MADAME.** Lucas, you taking notes? This boy's got the goods.

**BULRUSHER.** I don't need you. I don't need *you.* I might have, but now I got me this one. I got Vera. And I'm a take care a her.

**LOGGER.** That's different than what he's talking about Bulrush. She's your friend and he's talking romantic.

**MADAME.** But they standin too close together! I've seen this before, two girls stand too close, then they get distracted, and blow apart. If you're a woman, you can't fall in love, not with a man or with your friend. You just can't afford to. Schoolch, tell her.

*(**SCHOOLCH** is silent.)*

**BULRUSHER.** Vera will tell you. I'm a take care of her. I don't want nobody else.

**LOGGER.** Vera, what you say about all this?

**VERA.** She's a good friend.

**LOGGER.** That's all?

**BULRUSHER.** She kissed me. That's what I know. She kissed me and that means we are meant for each other, don't it?

**BOY.** You're a witch, a bulrusher, a colored girl, and a degenerate too? Oh I've got to save you with my songs of mercy. You don't want her, I'm tellin you you don't.

**LOGGER.** Vera, ain't there something you got to tell us?

**VERA.** I don't think so.

**LOGGER.** I realize it's early on and all so I've been letting you cavort and take in your last bit of childhood, but I know what you come here for. I'm up earlier than you, honey. I know you get tongue-cuppy in the mornings out back, and it's every morning, so I know. But we're still gonna get you to that college, believe you me.

**BOY.** You mean this girl is lizzied? Lews 'n larmers. Well congratulations to the man who got you heisted. See Bulrusher? That's just what I wanna do with you.

*(**BULRUSHER** punches **BOY**. They struggle.)*

**MADAME.** No upper-cuttin on my premises!

**LOGGER.** Let em fight it out. I wanna see who they are.

*(**BULRUSHER** is strong, but **BOY** is a more experienced fighter. He pins her arm behind her back and holds her down.)*

**BOY.** You still feel like hittin me?

**BULRUSHER.** Yes!

**VERA.** Stop it!

**BOY.** I'm asking you true, that's what you want?

**BULRUSHER.** Yes!

**BOY.** You think you can hurt me that way?

**BULRUSHER.** I hope so!

**BOY.** Then try.

*(He lets go and lies down, face up. She gets on top of him. A moment of reckoning – then she starts pummeling him.)*

**BULRUSHER.** *(punching with each word)* You. Don't. Want. Me.

**MADAME.** Lucas, I'll jump in there myself if you don't!

**BULRUSHER.** You. Don't Know Me.

**VERA.** He's bleeding!

**BULRUSHER.** He's drunk, he won't even notice.

**MADAME.** Bulrusher, stop this now!

*(**BULRUSHER** continues to hit him, focus intensified.)*

**VERA.** Why are you doing this?

**MADAME.** You may not listen, but you can feel.

*(**MADAME** tries to drag **BULRUSHER** off of him but **BULRUSHER** hits **MADAME**, knocking her to the floor.)*

**SCHOOLCH.** Bulrusher.

*(At the sound of his soft voice, everything stops.)*

**SCHOOLCH.** That's enough.

*(**SCHOOLCH** and **LOGGER** both move to help **MADAME** – an awkward moment that evolves into a silent showdown. Finally, **LOGGER** helps her up. **BULRUSHER** gets off of **BOY** slowly and stands, suddenly aware of what she has done.)*

**SCHOOLCH.** Go home, Bulrusher.

*(**BULRUSHER** looks at **VERA**, then runs out, driving off in her truck. **MADAME** is already cleaning.)*

**LOGGER.** Madame, you hurt?

**MADAME.** I'm mad, that's all. Look at the blood on my floor.

**LOGGER.** You alright son? Ooh, she Joe Macked you.

**BOY.** Got a tooth loose.

*(**MADAME** hands him a hot towel.)*

**MADAME.** Here's some brandy if you need it.

*(He drinks some.)*

**BOY.** I hope Bulrusher will forgive me. You think she will?

**LOGGER.** I'll take you home, Boy. Let's go Vera.

**MADAME.** What do you want a baby for.

**LOGGER.** Let's go.

*(**LOGGER, VERA,** and **BOY** exit.)*

*(Split scene: **MADAME** and **SCHOOLCH** continue to talk in the brothel parlor while **BULRUSHER** talks to the river.)*

**MADAME.** Damn babies. They grow up and make more. Grow up and serve nothing but hurt. Why did you take that girl in?

**BULRUSHER.** I float in a basket toward the Pacific, hands blue as huckleberries.

**MADAME.** How did Lucas find her in the weeds? Why did he bring that weese here?

**BULRUSHER.** The woman who bore me named me silence.

**MADAME.** He knew a baby in a brothel takes away more customers than war. The girls would hear her squall and remember they're women.

**BULRUSHER.** Who is a motherless daughter but pure will?

**MADAME.** She seemed like she was trying to fit in, but now she's a walking curse. Why did you take her in?

**BULRUSHER.** I want to swing, swing, over the green grapes, the fir trees, ride the wind, find my home, go all the way home.

**SCHOOLCH.** When your mother passed, you left town. You left me, you left Lucas.

**BULRUSHER.** Home.

**SCHOOLCH.** You stayed away a long time, but you came back.

**BULRUSHER.** Home. And I am…

**SCHOOLCH.** You know how I feel about you. Why'd you come back? Was it for me? Or him?

**BULRUSHER.** Who?

**SCHOOLCH.** Me? Or him?

**BULRUSHER.** Who.

**SCHOOLCH.** And who are you leaving now? Me? Or him.

**BULRUSHER.** Who?

**SCHOOLCH.** Madame? You answer me!

*(Long pause.)*

**MADAME.** There's blood on my floor.

*(Split scene ends – lights out on* **BULRUSHER**. **MADAME** *stoops to clean up the floor with her towel, but* **SCHOOLCH** *takes it and wipes the floor for her. He hands her the bloody towel.)*

**SCHOOLCH.** Cory up there?

**MADAME.** She's in the front with the men on the monthly plan. What, you want me to send her up?

**SCHOOLCH.** On the Wabash Cannonball.

*(He throws ten dollars on the pool table and goes up the stairs.* **MADAME**, *shocked, sits.)*

*(Next morning.* **BULRUSHER** *enters the brothel.* **MADAME** *has not moved since the night before. )*

**BULRUSHER.** Mornin.

**MADAME.** Looks the same to me.

**BULRUSHER.** I can open your shades for you.

**MADAME.** No thanks. Don't need any more heat in this room. And that sun bleaches my upholstery.

**BULRUSHER.** You seen Schoolch? I been worried. Couldn't sleep.

**MADAME.** Me neither.

**BULRUSHER.** He didn't come home last night.

**MADAME.** Don't trouble yourself about him.

**BULRUSHER.** You know where he is?

**MADAME.** He's here.

**BULRUSHER.** Here? Upstairs?

**MADAME.** That's right. Historic, ain't it? Schoolch finally getting his equipment serviced.

**BULRUSHER.** He – he really –

**MADAME.** Yes. It is natural, you know.

**BULRUSHER.** It's my fault. I'm sorry.

**MADAME.** It ain't your fault. Ain't your fault at all.

**BULRUSHER.** He's never gonna come home now. He's punishing me.

**MADAME.** You don't know that.

**BULRUSHER.** It's because of what I said and did last night that's pushed him over –

**MADAME.** No, child, he's punishing *me.*

**BULRUSHER.** Why?

**MADAME.** We've known each other a long long time. Know things about the other no one else knows. He's just angry that I'm leavin town.

**BULRUSHER.** You say you're leavin every summer.

**MADAME.** Well maybe he was mad at me for being so easy on you! When you knocked me over, you cracked my porcelain spittoon!

**BULRUSHER.** I apologize for that too.

**MADAME.** You better!

**BULRUSHER.** I mean to work it all off. Maybe I can help you with your business here, take in some clients for you.

**MADAME.** What? Work a bed for me?

**BULRUSHER.** I mean – well, during the Apple Show – if you're short staffed.

**MADAME.** You ain't even had your cherry popped.

**BULRUSHER.** What do you mean?

**MADAME.** My point exactly. You can't just fling yourself into this profession! It's gotta be part of a plan. And I don't want you disrespecting the solicitors I represent with your lack of training and experience. You'd probably get knocked up, like that Vera girl, the love of your life.

**BULRUSHER.** You don't know how I feel about her.

**MADAME.** I know she's a girl. And she's pregnant. Soon she'll be a woman, with a baby, and she's gonna need more than you can give.

**BULRUSHER.** What can't I give? You think she want somebody who talk all that talk about "you are my for sure" like Boy did last night? He's probably been practicing them lines on every girl he know for the last ten years. He'd say that to a whore.

*(**MADAME**'s look stops **BULRUSHER** cold.)*

**BULRUSHER.** *(explains)* You don't know what that Boy and his friends used to do to me.

**MADAME.** He's trying to give something to you and she's trying to take something from you. You got to choose wisely.

**BULRUSHER.** You're just sticking up for him 'cause you're both white people.

**MADAME.** That girl has put so much hate into you. *(pause)* You shouldn't see her for a little while.

**BULRUSHER.** Did you talk to her?

**MADAME.** I talked to Lucas. He called this morning.

**BULRUSHER.** What'd he say?

**MADAME.** Said you needed to cool off.

**BULRUSHER.** I am cool.

**MADAME.** You meant to hurt Boy last night, and you did.

**BULRUSHER.** But Boy don't care what I do. Nothing I do can change him.

**MADAME.** That's just not how you treat people.

**BULRUSHER.** I'm sorry. I did it for Vera.

**MADAME.** And you better cool offa her too.

**BULRUSHER.** Can't I apologize?

**MADAME.** Lucas don't want you seein Vera no more.

**BULRUSHER.** I don't need to kiss her, that was what she did to me. Once. We can just talk.

**MADAME.** He says no.

**BULRUSHER.** But I said I'd take care of her and the boy when he's born.

**MADAME.** A boy?

**BULRUSHER.** I read her water. It was an accident.

**MADAME.** What do you want with her baby?

**BULRUSHER.** I ain't never had a family. So maybe with her, I can make my own.

**MADAME.** I've got to have clean lines in my life, nothing blurry: gotta keep all the food on my plate in separate heaps, can't put on my knickers if they haven't been ironed. Anything unexpected, anything messy, I clean it up. My path has always been clear in front of me... but I can't see it anymore. Somebody wants to buy this place for more money than I ever expected to see in my life, and I should be happy, but between that and you and Lucas and Schoolch I feel like something's choking me... I want that man, but how can I have him?... There's something I'm supposed to do but I don't know what it is. Do you?

**BULRUSHER.** You're shaking, Madame.

**MADAME.** I feel like I'm having a greeney. I need to know something. I need to know what I'm supposed to do.

**BULRUSHER.** Why are you asking me?

*(**MADAME** walks into the kitchen and brings back a bowl of water. )*

**MADAME.** Can't you see it on my face? I'm not breathing right. Nothing I plant ever grows in my garden... If I could just smell the grass on my mother's grave, smell the grass growing there –

**BULRUSHER.** What for?

*(**MADAME** plunges her hands into the bowl and splashes water onto her face.)*

**MADAME.** Read my water.

**BULRUSHER.** Schoolch.

**MADAME.** I'll worry about him.

**BULRUSHER.** I said I wouldn't read again, unless Vera wanted me to.

**MADAME.** I need you to tell me what to do. Tell me what to do.

**BULRUSHER.** I want to see Vera.

**MADAME.** I told you Lucas said no.

**BULRUSHER.** I'll read your water if you arrange for us to meet.

**MADAME.** You can't love that girl!

**BULRUSHER.** Call him. Or I won't read.

*(**MADAME** picks up the phone to call **LOGGER**. She begins to cry as she talks.)*

**MADAME.** Lucas, how you doin. No, I'm fine, was just calling about Vera. She's got to get over to the doctor, you know. Make sure she and that baby are alright. I can take her when I go into Mendocino. No, I'll do it. I've done it before. She needs a woman around for that kind of thing. Enough lying on a cold metal table and showing yourself to a man with bad breath. What? No, nothing's wrong with me. No, I'm not crying. It's just hot in here. I'll call you later.

*(She hangs up.)*

**MADAME.** There.

*(She moves the bowl of water to **BULRUSHER**.)*

**BULRUSHER.** Don't let Vera get rid of the baby.

**MADAME.** Don't push it. I asked you to read my water, not hers.

**BULRUSHER.** I can't guarantee I'll see something you want to see.

**MADAME.** Just hurry.

**BULRUSHER.** This could be like May Bloyd.

**MADAME.** May had that coming to her. She wasn't the saint she made herself out to be.

**BULRUSHER.** If you cry, cry over the bowl, I'll get a stronger signal that way.

**MADAME.** Can you see the past?

**BULRUSHER.** Water has a current. I follow where it goes. Hands in the water.

*(***BULRUSHER** *puts her hands into the water with* **MADAME***'s. She closes her eyes. After several beats, she pulls* **MADAME***'s hands out, holding them over the bowl.* **SCHOOLCH** *comes down the stairs, unseen.)*

**BULRUSHER.** Don't see anything but you in a blue hat.

**MADAME.** That's it?

**BULRUSHER.** Yeah – it just looks all the same from here on. Two pillows on your bed, and a blue hat.

**MADAME.** That's how soon from now?

*(***BULRUSHER** *opens her eyes.)*

**BULRUSHER.** I don't get time, I get pictures. That's the only one coming through.

**MADAME.** How is that supposed to help me? You sure ain't what you advertise.

**SCHOOLCH.** Mornin.

*(***BULRUSHER** *drops* **MADAME***'s hands, drying her own on her clothes.)*

**BULRUSHER.** Mornin. I came to find you.

**MADAME.** Schoolch, she didn't see nothin.

**SCHOOLCH.** You asked her to read when you know she's wiped her hands of fortune?

**MADAME.** How can she wipe her hands of themselves?

**SCHOOLCH.** You don't mind them calling her a witch then. Well I do. You ain't never loved her. Never loved anybody. Well I do.

**BULRUSHER.** I made you some spoonbread, Schoolch. I didn't know where you were.

**SCHOOLCH.** I was setting myself free. You can't be bound to people who don't know how to love.

**BULRUSHER.** You didn't come home. Don't do that again without telling me.

(**SCHOOLCH** *laughs.* **BULRUSHER** *smiles.)*

**MADAME.** Schoolch. I don't know what I'm supposed to do.

(**SCHOOLCH** *pulls out a leather envelope thick with money.)*

**SCHOOLCH.** This should help.

**MADAME.** *(pulling money from envelope, realizing)* You wrote me that letter? *You* wanna buy me out? Why?

**SCHOOLCH.** I want you to leave. I don't care if it costs my life savings. If you ain't gonna set things right, you gotta leave. I'm tired of waitin and I'm tired of bein tired. Make up your mind.

(**SCHOOLCH** *and* **BULRUSHER** *exit.* **MADAME** *sits.)*

*(Lights change. The river. One week later.* **BULRUSHER** *and* **VERA** *are in the water, making love. In the staging, they are not actually touching, but can feel every movement made by the other.* **BULRUSHER** *speaks to the river.* **VERA** *cannot hear her.)*

**BULRUSHER.** Pampas grass, Swiss chard,
waterfall, chipmunk.
And vines, vines, growing in the hill.

Monkeyflower and jackrabbits,
a roll dipped in apricot jam,
fresh cream turns to butter in the churn.

I swing, swing, over the poppies,
the scrub pine: I'm a meteor, its trail,
hold a star on my tongue.

*(They come out of the water and begin putting their clothes back on. They are strangely awkward with each other – their lovemaking wasn't what they thought it would be.* **VERA** *is a bit faraway;* **BULRUSHER** *looks to her for cues.)*

**VERA.** Hey.

**BULRUSHER.** Hey.

**VERA.** I missed you.

**BULRUSHER.** You got a new dress.

**VERA.** Madame gave it to me. I put it on in the doctor's office. I guess I'm supposed to grow into it.

**BULRUSHER.** So the baby's… ?

**VERA.** Still there.

**BULRUSHER.** Good. Does your uncle talk bad about me?

**VERA.** Mainly he sings songs to my stomach. He's been real nice to me.

**BULRUSHER.** He's a good man.

**VERA.** He made friends with a long distance operator and called my mother. Now she knows everything.

**BULRUSHER.** Are you going back?

*(Pause.)*

**VERA.** A white man did this to me. A policeman. I typed reports for him in the front office.

**BULRUSHER.** Do you love him?

**VERA.** He raped me. And my boyfriend is studying to be a pastor.

**BULRUSHER.** Do you want me to kill him?

**VERA.** That's so sweet.

**BULRUSHER.** Then I'll do it.

**VERA.** I don't want him dead, I want him to change. *(to herself)* All of em gotta change…

**BULRUSHER.** I thought you wanted all white people murdered. I'd do that for you. As many as I could.

**VERA.** Bulrusher, don't say that. I was just talking.

**BULRUSHER.** Maybe the same thing happened to you happened to my mother. Maybe that's why she got rid of me.

**VERA.** No, I can tell you were made from love. So you shouldn't go beating people up.

**BULRUSHER.** We've saved up a lot of money. That plus the Apple Show, we can go away somewhere. Drive the truck down to Mexico. No one will know where the baby comes from.

**VERA.** And you'd leave Schoolch?

**BULRUSHER.** I'd have food sent to him from the hotel.

**VERA.** But you'd be okay without him?

**BULRUSHER.** Mm hm.

**VERA.** He's white, you could just kill him.

**BULRUSHER.** I could.

**VERA.** *(laughing)* You couldn't. You sure don't know how to lie.

**BULRUSHER.** Is your boyfriend gonna be mad that you ran off with me?

**VERA.** Fred? He doesn't get mad, he prays. "What you do to the least you do to me," something like that. And sometimes he believes the things he says. At least I hope so. What about Boy? He's gonna be awful teary if you go.

**BULRUSHER.** I don't understand him. His friends used to lift up my shirt and wouldn't let me go till I said I had goat titties. Boy wouldn't do nothing but watch and laugh. Now I'm the sparkle of his eye?

**VERA.** Well you probably *did* have goat titties back then. You don't anymore.

**BULRUSHER.** Isn't that the same as what the policeman did to you?

**VERA.** You already broke the boy's face in, what else do you want?

*(**MADAME** enters.)*

**MADAME.** You still have your clothes on, that's good news. Wrap it up now, I don't want to put Lucas on the wonder.

**VERA.** Just a few more minutes, ma'am.

**MADAME.** You want me to wait until you go into labor? I got things to do.

**VERA.** We won't be long.

**MADAME.** I'm going to sit in the car. Don't make me have to come and get you again.

**BULRUSHER.** A few more minutes.

*(**MADAME** exits.)*

**BULRUSHER.** Should we take off our clothes again just to show her?

**VERA.** No.

**BULRUSHER.** I did get that turpentine feeling under my skin again. But your lips were – cold.

**VERA.** What did you see when you kissed me? Did you see my future?

**BULRUSHER.** I thought I would, but I didn't. You were blurry, like when a person doesn't want me to read. Maybe kissing makes a different kind of water? 'Cause all I felt – was your mouth. Cold.

**VERA.** You didn't like it.

**BULRUSHER.** Um… I think so.

**VERA.** You didn't. I know you didn't. It's okay though. Find the right person I guess, and everything'll fall into place.

**BULRUSHER.** What about you? You could teach me.

**VERA.** There's feeling *(she places her hands over her own and* **BULRUSHER***'s heart)* and touching *(she palms* **BULRUSHER***'s hip).* Sometimes they both come in the same person and sometimes they don't. I think you like Boy. That's who you're meant for.

**BULRUSHER.** He's not pretty.

**VERA.** But he's cute.

**BULRUSHER.** And I said I'd take care of you.

**VERA.** Woman of your word.

**BULRUSHER.** Everything will be fine when we go away together. We'll just have to find a town with a river.

**VERA.** My mother sent the first Jet magazine I won.

**BULRUSHER.** And the pomade?

**VERA.** She kept that. There's a picture in here I want you to see.

*(***VERA** *shows her the magazine.)*

**BULRUSHER.** Is that a dead boy?

**VERA.** That's what the headline says.

**BULRUSHER.** But his head looks like a football with gravel glued on. There's no nose, eyes, mouth – he doesn't have a face left.

**VERA.** They killed him and drowned him in a river for whistling at a white woman.

**BULRUSHER.** This happened in your town?

**VERA.** Close enough.

**BULRUSHER.** Why do colored people even live where these things happen?

**VERA.** Because we're done runnin… done bein ashamed. We didn't do nothing wrong but get born.

**BULRUSHER.** Why didn't the river save him?

**VERA.** I guess so we could save ourselves. When I watched you beat that Boy up, I suddenly knew right then and there that I couldn't undo my own hurt by making more. One day I'm gonna be a teacher and I'm 'n a say what I know. That we can take our hate and let it open us so wide we can love anybody. That we can stand in the face of violence and say I can take that, I'm bigger than that.

**BULRUSHER.** Bigger than the white people.

**VERA.** Bigger than our own small fists.

**MADAME.** *(calling from offstage)* Vera now, let's move it.

**BULRUSHER.** So I'll see you at the Apple Show.

**VERA.** *(laughing)* We'll disappear after the dance. We'll drive off into the sunset, won't we?

**BULRUSHER.** And the love songs will come on the radio and they'll be about us.

*(**VERA** is silent.)*

**BULRUSHER.** Did *you* like it? Kissing me?

**VERA.** This is for you. Got it in Mendocino.

*(**VERA** hands **BULRUSHER** a small pewter hand mirror engraved with flowers.)*

**VERA.** I wanted to kiss you all over from the moment I met you. I don't know why. Never felt like that about a girl, ever. But then when we do kiss, it's like – it's like you said. It's cold, like I'm pressing my lips to a mirror, like it's just me again and again, over and over. I don't know why *that* is either. Each time, cold kisses, cold rain. *(touches **BULRUSHER**'s cheek)* And we can't do nothin about the weather. *(stands)* Just take this – and remember me when you look at your own face.

**BULRUSHER.** It's nice, but I don't need it. I'll be seeing you all the time.

**VERA.** Keep it anyway.

*(As* **VERA** *begins to leave, she leans down to the water and whispers to it.)*

**VERA.** *(to river, softly)* Thank you.

**BULRUSHER.** I'll meet you after the Apple Show dance.

**VERA.** Bulrusher.

**BULRUSHER.** What.

**VERA.** Don't learn how to lie.

*(Suddenly* **MADAME** *is there.)*

**MADAME.** *(to* **VERA***)* In the car.

*(***VERA** *hesitates, looking at* **BULRUSHER***. Then, she goes.)*

**MADAME.** *(to* **BULRUSHER***)* Bulrush, Schoolch says some-one's coming to see you.

**BULRUSHER.** Who?

**MADAME.** He says he heard from your mother, up by Clear Lake. She wants to do penance. Huh. Bout time. She'll meet you Sunday dusk by Wharf Rock.

**BULRUSHER.** My mother? But Sunday is the Apple Show dance.

**MADAME.** So? You want to meet her, don't you?

**BULRUSHER.** I guess.

**MADAME.** Sunday by Wharf Rock.

*(Lights change.* **BULRUSHER** *talks to the river as the Apple Show begins. Music.)*

**BULRUSHER.** Dusk, Sunday.
Dusk, Sunday.

Schoolch says my mother
will meet me: dusk,
Sunday, by Wharf Rock.

What will I do with
my hands? Will she push
me into the ocean?
Throw herself to the tide?

O river,
tell me, tell me:

will I kill her?

*(The Apple Show. Everyone dances as* **BOY** *calls it from the grandstand.* **MADAME** *leads* **LOGGER**, *who does not know how to dance, while* **SCHOOLCH** *and* **BULRUSHER** *dance with great flourish. Stomping, clapping.)*

**BOY.** Headgents give right hands across and balance four in line
Back with the left and don't get lost and mind your steps and time
Swing your partner halfway round and balance there again
Swing your partner to her place and those two ladies chain
Rat a tat tat, rat a tat tat, rat a tat tat
Rat a tat tat, rat a tat tat, rat a tat tat

**LOGGER.** I told you you'd stay for the dance.

**MADAME.** Only because you said you'd come.

**LOGGER.** Can't believe you actually drug me to a dance. I don't do things I ain't good at.

**MADAME.** You're tripping over your shoelaces pretty well.

*(They dance.* **BULRUSHER**, *now in her booth, reads water for unseen townspeople.)*

**BULRUSHER.** It's 50 cents for one image of your future. Please pay before you place your hand in the water sir. Thank you. Relax your arm. Alright. *(a few beats)* Your sheep are going to be attacked by bobcats. Next.

*(***BOY** *walks up.)*

**BOY.** Will you tell our future?

**BULRUSHER.** Step aside, I'm only taking paying customers. It's 50 cents, ma'am.

**BOY.** I want you to be in my future.

**BULRUSHER.** Let me get this bowl refreshed.

**BOY.** I wrote songs for you and everything.

**BULRUSHER.** Relax your arm. You will purchase a pair of socks that are very intriguing to a person whose sex is difficult to ascertain. No, thank *you.*

**BOY.** You're still sore over hitting me the other night?

**BULRUSHER.** You'd like two dollars worth of images? Yes sir, I'll give you your money's worth – and add one more for free!

**BOY.** You got my jaw real good. I can't eat any of these crunchy apples.

**BULRUSHER.** Very relaxed arm, that's a good sign. Your gonorrhea will clear up and be less of a hindrance in your adultery. You will oversleep and miss your mother's funeral. You will leave the Anyhow Saloon drunk and crash your truck into Petrified Gulch, where your tires will calcify before you can tow it out. You will – you sure? But you get two more, we ain't done. Well at least take a complimentary navel orange.

**BOY.** I know I can't make up your mind for you, but won't you give me a little somethin?

**BULRUSHER.** I'm working, Boy. And then I'm leaving.

**BOY.** How bout a dance before you go?

**BULRUSHER.** Just stop bothering me! Look, I'm sorry I broke in your face.

**BOY.** I'm sorry for not talking to you till – lately.

**BULRUSHER.** And.

**BOY.** I'm sorry for not putting my arm around you in the Anyhow.

**BULRUSHER.** And.

**BOY.** I'm sorry for laughing at your goat titties.

**BULRUSHER.** So we're square. Listen, I've got to get to Wharf Rock by dusk but I need you to keep an eye out for Vera.

**BOY.** You're still stuck on her.

**BULRUSHER.** I'm taking care of her.

**BOY.** That's different. Means I still got a chance. Did you ever read that love letter I wrote you when we was twelve?

**BULRUSHER.** I took it to the outhouse and threw it down.

**BOY.** *(smiles)* I always knew you liked me.

**BULRUSHER.** Tell Vera to wait for me if you see her.

**BOY.** If you'll give me a dance.

**BULRUSHER.** Trade.

**BOY.** *(a whoop)* Eeeee tah! What you going to Wharf Rock for?

**BULRUSHER.** To meet my mother.

(**SCHOOLCH** *walks up to* **BULRUSHER***'s booth.)*

**BOY.** Afternoon. Bulrusher's gonna dance with me.

(**BOY** *walks away.* **BULRUSHER** *starts to gather up her money.)*

**BULRUSHER.** Schoolch.

**SCHOOLCH.** Bulrush.

**BULRUSHER.** You mind me reading fortunes?

**SCHOOLCH.** No, never. Just minded what all these people had to say about you when you did.

**BULRUSHER.** I can take it.

**SCHOOLCH.** I believe you.

**BULRUSHER.** Thanks for taking care of me Schoolch.

**SCHOOLCH.** So you're gonna kill your mother and run off with Vera. You got your majority, you can do what you want. I just wanted to make sure that was your plan.

**BULRUSHER.** I was gonna have your food sent from the hotel.

**SCHOOLCH.** Where's the shotgun.

**BULRUSHER.** I'll bring it back. I'm just afraid she's gonna try and kill me again.

**SCHOOLCH.** You didn't need that gun when you were a baby.

**BULRUSHER.** Why did she say we had to meet by the ocean? That's where she sent me to die. I've never been there and I don't want to go. If I even look at the ocean, it might take away all my river power – it could still kill me.

**SCHOOLCH.** You can tell everybody else's fortunes, but you could never tell your own.

(**SCHOOLCH** *watches* **MADAME** *and* **LOGGER** *dance.* **MADAME** *notices him and stops, leaving her hand in* **LOGGER***'s.* **SCHOOLCH** *bows to her, and exits.* **MADAME** *and* **LOGGER** *begin to dance again with* **BULRUSHER** *and* **BOY**.)

**MADAME.** Fancy footwork, Boy. Keep it loose 'cause she might split your lip on the next beat.

**LOGGER.** Mm, she's starting to look reformed to me. Got a sense of purpose about her.

**MADAME.** You want her to read your fortune?

**LOGGER.** Nope. Holding it right here in my hands.

(**MADAME** *and* **LOGGER** *dance off the stage.*)

**BOY.** Schoolch taught you all this?

**BULRUSHER.** Yup. He even gets a periodical sent to him from Kansas City with pictures of the new steps.

**BOY.** Let me hold you like this. *(he puts his hand on her hip)* Your hip feels kinda hard. Is that all the money you made?

**BULRUSHER.** And saved. What. You don't like how hard work feels?

**BOY.** Well maybe if you'd just – dance a little closer. A little slower. Yeah, like that.

(**BULRUSHER** *moves in and takes his tempo for a few measures. Fireworks – but this time, inside them. She stops dancing.*)

**BULRUSHER.** Alright, that's enough.

**BOY.** You liked dancing with me! I could feel it.

**BULRUSHER.** Keep an eye for Vera. And Boy –

(**BULRUSHER** *kisses him on the cheek. Then she walks away.* **BOY** *hops onto the grandstand.*)

**BOY.** And this song is for Boonville's own Bulrusher, who has come out of early retirement to tell our fortunes again. I don't know about you, but doesn't that make you feel more secure? Ain't it swell to know where you're going?

*(stomping and clapping again, he calls:)*

Apples in a pot
Apples in a pot
Skin is getting hot
Skin is getting hot
Lemon
sugar
brown

*(Wharf Rock. Ocean waves crashing.* **BULRUSHER** *hugs the shotgun to herself. She is unsteady and chants to tame the ocean of her nerves.)*

**BULRUSHER.** *(eyes closed)* Seaspray,
dress me in white mist,
hide me from her.

*(No response from the ocean.)*

Seaspray, white mist,
clothe me in salt.

*(No response. She opens her eyes.)*

You're not like the river. You
won't listen. But you will not have me.
You are the mother I refuse.

I will live, and live,
live, and live,
without the terror of your love.

*(***MADAME*** appears in a blue hat.)*

**MADAME.** We don't look nothing alike.

*(***BULRUSHER*** spins around to her.)*

**BULRUSHER.** Blue hat.

**MADAME.** Is that gun for me?

**BULRUSHER.** Madame.

**MADAME.** Yeah. Don't call me anything different.

**BULRUSHER.** Madame.

**MADAME.** A gun. Where'd you get all these violent impulses?

**BULRUSHER.** Madame?

**MADAME.** Yeah. *(pause)* Well don't stand there dumb, let's us have a conversation. Ain't you saved up some questions for me?

*(Pause.)*

**BULRUSHER.** No.

**MADAME.** I know you got some curiosity.

*(Pause.)*

**BULRUSHER.** When you leaving?

**MADAME.** You know I say that every summer when the heat gets to me. Gave Schoolch his money back. I can't leave none a you. So you glad it's me? Coulda been someone you couldn't relate to, somebody lacking morals and accountability.

**BULRUSHER.** I just – what you –

**MADAME.** Spit it out.

**BULRUSHER.** How could – I don't – this ocean air is trying to kill me –

**MADAME.** No it ain't. You can talk.

**BULRUSHER.** I don't got any questions. I got to go.

**MADAME.** Bulrush, hold on. We don't gotta change nothing, let's just talk a while.

**BULRUSHER.** I got to go. Vera.

**MADAME.** I still have that basket I wove you. Went down and picked it up after Lucas found you. Wove it from reeds and rushes I found near Clear Lake when my ma was sick. You kept growin in me, she passed, then you were born. Thought it would be nice for you to float in that basket and look up at the sky. But I was greedy. I had to spend a while with you before I sent you off; had to see what of Lucas made it into you.

**BULRUSHER.** Vera and I are cousins?

**MADAME.** Kiss kiss.

**BULRUSHER.** I've got to tell her.

**MADAME.** Bulrush –

**BULRUSHER.** I'm going!

*(**MADAME** grabs **BULRUSHER** by the shoulders.)*

**MADAME.** Lucas took Vera to the train. She's going back to Birmingham.

**BULRUSHER.** I can catch her.

**MADAME.** No you can't.

**BULRUSHER.** Why not?

**MADAME.** The train left yesterday.

**BULRUSHER.** What about the baby.

**MADAME.** What about it. It's up to her.

*(**BULRUSHER** pulls all the money out of her pockets and throws it into the ocean.)*

**MADAME.** Now what did you do that for?

**BULRUSHER.** You made Vera go away.

**MADAME.** No.

**BULRUSHER.** You sent me down the river like I wasn't nothing but shorn hair. White whore didn't want her colored baby.

**MADAME.** I ain't white, my ma's a Pomo Indian. The rest I hope you'll let me make up for.

**BULRUSHER.** I always wished you were my ma. But why should I want you now?

**MADAME.** You don't have to.

**BULRUSHER.** I got plenty of shame. Plenty. And now you want to scrape some more off your shoe and rub it on me. You ain't nothing. Nothing but shame.

**MADAME.** That's right. Think my mother wanted me to be a businesswoman? Think I could have kept my business with folks knowing I was Indian? I made my choice, stuck to it by her deathbed. Wasn't going to put you through all that I knew. Wasn't going to have no customer's baby. And I wasn't tryin to lose no customer named Lucas.

**BULRUSHER.** You told Lucas the truth, that I'm his?

**MADAME.** No, I told him I would marry him.

**BULRUSHER.** He wouldn't marry you if he knew about me.

**MADAME.** I guess I wanted to clear it with you – see if you want another father.

**BULRUSHER.** I ain't givin up Schoolch.

**MADAME.** You don't have to.

**BULRUSHER.** You already turned Schoolch down. He should have somebody in this world.

**MADAME.** He has what he's always had. I wish I wanted Schoolch, 'cause he never wanted to be a customer. And he never used you against me. Raised you with pure intent, followed you like a calling.

**BULRUSHER.** *You* didn't follow *me* down the river, I did that by myself.

**MADAME.** What do you want me to say?

**BULRUSHER.** I want you to apologize for trying to kill me.

**MADAME.** I didn't want you dead.

**BULRUSHER.** Then why did you get rid of me like that? I was floating for an eternity.

**MADAME.** You can't remember that.

**BULRUSHER.** Yes I can. Yes I can. I remember floating in the night, the fog and the coyotes – didn't know what that sound was then but I do now. Mr Jeans found me at Barney Flats, but I was there for days. I begged to be found. I talked to the sun with my fingers, kept closing my fist around it every time it went down trying to keep it with me. But the night would always come. And the river was so thin there, deep as a teardrop – but I kept myself alive. Why? To find you? To lose the only one who ever really touched me? Schoolch never did, he doesn't know how. Only told me to sit up straight. Vera touched me, gave me softness and you made her leave. You knew she was going when I saw her last, didn't you. *(***MADAME** *is silent.)* Of course you did. So is she gonna kill the baby or be the preacher's wife who got raped by a cop?

**MADAME.** You're angry with me.

**BULRUSHER.** I'm not angry. I'm gonna kill you. I want to kill something. Walk toward the edge of that bluff. Do it.

*(***MADAME** *doesn't move and* **BULRUSHER** *aims her shotgun.)*

**BULRUSHER.** Back to me. Go to the ocean and look at it.

*(***MADAME** *walks to the edge of the cliff.)*

**BULRUSHER.** See it gnashing its teeth? It wants you. Didn't want me. But it still wants to eat. Salt gonna sting your eyes, gonna burn you. All that seaweed down there is gonna grab you and drown you.

**MADAME.** Bulrusher.

**BULRUSHER.** You already dead, ever since you tried to kill me. You been dead.

**MADAME.** Bulrush –

**BULRUSHER.** Dead for money. Wanted some damn money steada me. Well go get it. I threw it in there for you. It's all yours.

**MADAME.** Bulrusher, I named you.

**BULRUSHER.** Bulrusher, caught in the bulrushes, abandoned to the weeds. I'm a weed.

**MADAME.** You got a name. You ain't a weed.

**BULRUSHER.** Jeans? Whore? Sneeble? Witch?

**MADAME.** You got my mama's name. You got your grandma's name just like she wanted you to have it.

**BULRUSHER.** Pomo? Indian? I don't want it.

**MADAME.** You got her name. It's Xa-wena. Means on the water.

**BULRUSHER.** You called me that once. One day.

**MADAME.** You remember.

**BULRUSHER.** I remember everything.

**MADAME.** *(chants softly in Pomo)* O beda-Xa, a thi shishkith, ometh ele'le'. Xa-wéna ewé-ba ke katsilith'ba ele'ledith. O beda-Xa, a thi boshtotsith.

*(speaks)* River water, I ask you, protect her, help her. Take her to your bosom. Save her from the night and cold, river water, protect her. I thank you.

*(***MADAME** *turns around.* **BULRUSHER** *has lowered her shotgun.)*

I prayed for you in your basket. And your river listened. She listened. The river's your mother. I throw stones into it everyday to thank her for caring for you.

*(***MADAME** *kneels and hugs* **BULRUSHER***'s legs.)*

**MADAME.** See? I got softness.

*(Pause.)*

**BULRUSHER.** Xa-wena.

**MADAME.** Yes?

**BULRUSHER.** I was just sayin it.

**MADAME.** Oh.

*(Lights fade.* **MADAME** *exits. Spot on* **BULRUSHER** *holding the mirror* **VERA** *gave her. She can barely speak as she tries to find her bearings in the things she knows.)*

**BULRUSHER.** Chaparral, dust, frogs, cicadas, bay trees, sequoias, pine cones, horse shit, lizards, hummingbirds, ravines, ferns, eucalyptus, woodchips, wild rose, full moon in clouds, exposed roots, skunks, hawks, poppies, driftwood fences, yellow hills, cormorants, spiderwebs, all blown dandelion zero.

*(Two weeks later.* **BULRUSHER** *sits on the porch with* **SCHOOLCH**. *During the following lines,* **LOGGER** *enters and puts his foot up on the porch.* **BULRUSHER** *does not talk to the river, but to the audience. She is easy, calm.)*

**BULRUSHER.** This town is a byway, a traveler's raincoat
folded away from sight. People need
something stop here. They smell it, take it,

and pass through. I sell oranges, balls
of sun. You eat them in sections like a heart
torn from the spine. When they're gone,

I lie in my red flatbed and watch the stars
fall without pity.

**LOGGER.** *(lively)* So Madame and I talkin bout getting locked real soon, October, when the sun fades some and we can have a party in her garden. Both of you invited of course, I'll even braid your hair special Bulrush if you want me to.

**BULRUSHER.** Schoolch and I smoke cigarettes
by the duck pond, I peel bark
from the madrone tree and rub
the smooth beneath.

**LOGGER.** Schoolch, hope you don't mind that I won Madame after all these years you been courtin. But you know, the woman's got her own mind and well, she made it up. Two pillows on her bed now. And Bulrush, you got every right to stay on here with Schoolch, but you just let me know if you need anything, not that Schoolch wouldn't already have it to give, but you know, if you need anything, uh, the family history and so forth, I got a lot a stories, uh, diseases you might be prone to, uh, and the like, of that nature.

**BULRUSHER.** Soon it will be colder than ever.
In the garden my collards will be pregnant with ice.
But an early frost makes the greens taste sweeter.

**LOGGER.** You woulda died in them weeds if I hadn't found ya. And then Schoolch was good enough to raise you up. Well, can't judge Madame for what never happened. *(bright)* Got a letter today, from Birmingham. Your cousin Vera wrote you a note. I hear she's gettin married soon too.

*(He gives the letter to* **BULRUSHER***.)*

Gotta have you a family and a church to lean on in a city like that. It's just been sounding worse and worse down there ever since that boy got… what they did to him… But you can't just take what pain life has to give you, you gotta make something out of it too. People see you got that kinda strength, they can't deny you. No sirree.

**SCHOOLCH.** When I finally took away Bulrusher's bottle she cried and cried all night. 'I want my bah-ul! I want my bah-ul!' Come the next morning she didn't need it no more. But she had turned and turned so in the crib her hair got matted into chunks. It was like she had a hat on made of steel wool. I tried to comb through it, poured baby oil all over it, dunked her in a big vat of lard, but those tangles wouldn't come out.

**LOGGER.** Is that the truth.

**SCHOOLCH.** So I had to cut it all off. Cut it all off.

*(Pause.)*

**LOGGER.** Did you. *(laughing)* Well Bulrusher you must have cried all that next night too!

*(***LOGGER*** hugs* **BULRUSHER** *with one arm.)*

**SCHOOLCH.** She did. I sat by her crib. Didn't hold her but she knew I was there.

*(***BULRUSHER*** looks at* **SCHOOLCH,** *then puts the letter into a bowl of water. She lifts up the paper and lets the ink run. She sinks the letter back in, and tries to get a signal. Nothing. She pulls her hands out, then puts them back in. Nothing. Once more she tries, hands in – )*

**LOGGER.** So how is Vera?

**BULRUSHER.** I can't tell.

*(Her hands are still in the water.)*

**LOGGER.** Oh, you don't read off of paper. Uh huh.

**BULRUSHER.** No, anything somebody touch I can read from once it's in water. Maybe I can't read *her* anymore. Or maybe I can't read at all.

**LOGGER.** Now don't say "can't." You can do anything you want if you put your mind to it. Schoolch, you thought about installing a phone here? I put one in and now I can't live without it.

*(***BOY*** enters, plucking his guitar. He sits next to* **BULRUSHER.***)*

**BOY.** I got a new song for you.

**BULRUSHER.** I got a new name.

**BOY.** What is it?

*(***BULRUSHER*** pulls her hands out of the bowl, turns it onto its rim and lets the water run out. She looks at* **BOY** *gently. Blackout.)*

**END OF PLAY**

## A GLOSSARY FOR THE CURIOUS

from *Boontling: An American Lingo* by Charles C. Adams, Mountain House Press, 1990

*Bulrusher* foundling, illegitimate child
*Navarro* Bulrusher's river; main waterway west to the ocean
*high shams* thick brush
*Schoolch* short for school teacher
*hobbin* dancing
*flattened* sick
*flag's out* menstruating
*geechin* penetration
*bow for* have sex with *(bow is pronounced like a violin bow)*
*burlap* have sex with
*bahl* good
*stringy hair and wrinkle socks* an unkempt woman
*moldunes* breasts
*pike* road
*madges* prostitutes
*heel scratchin* sex
*rout* scold
*harp* talk
*that's earth* that's the truth
*sulled* angered
*dehigged* broke, without money
*jackers* young men who masturbate
*dish* cheat
*can-kicky* angry
*buzzchick* baseball
*bookers* black people
*silent seeker* quiet, unobtrusive seducer
*shike* beat someone in a deal *(rhymes with "like")*
*booker tee* black man
*nonch harpin* dirty talk
*Fourth of Jeel* Fourth of July
*cocked darley* habitually angry
*moshe* automobile *(rhymes with "gauche")*
*ling* Boontling
*mossy* change the subject
*bilchin* having sex with
*Philo* a neighboring rival town *(pronounced FY-low)*
*tarp* pudendum of either sex
*boarch* Chinese male
*ink-standy* tired
*applehead* girl, girlfriend
*roger* storm
*mink* woman *(of easy morals, well dressed enough to afford mink)*
*fiddlers* delirium tremens

*put in on* to court
*ricky chow* sexual intercourse
*pearlin* raining
*cut cabbage* a black woman, the feeling of her vagina
*gorm* food
*scottied* hungry
*flories* biscuits
*toobs* two bits, a quarter
*belhoon* a dollar
*rooje* cheat *(pronounced like "rouge")*
*horn and chiggle* food and drink *(the verb "horn" means "to drink")*
*tidrey* a little bit
*jape* drive
*jenny* snitch
*jimhead* confused
*tuddish* mentally disabled *(same vowels as "rubbish")*
*ear settin* a lecture
*somersettin* to become emotionally upset
*comb's gettin red* puberty
*dubs* double
*sneeble* black person
*highgun* shotgun
*teet lipped* angry
*dove cooey* lonely
*golden eagles* underwear *(made from Golden Eagle brand flour sacks)*
*doolsey boo* sweet potato
*hoot* laugh
*whittlin* politicking
*warblin* singing
*yink* young man
*jonnems* tall tales
*wess* exaggerate
*airtight* no problem, also name for a sawmill
*grizz* old bachelor
*tweed* child
*daming* womanizing
*chucks* dull or unruly children
*skee* whiskey
*barlow* pocketknife
*ridgy* backwoodsy
*bloocher* one who chatters aimlessly or masturbates
*tongue-cuppy* nauseous, to vomit
*lizzied* pregnant
*lews 'n larmers* gossip
*heisted* pregnant
*upper-cuttin* fist fight
*Joe Mack* to beat someone up
*weese* infant
*greeney* a fit, a strange feeling associated with sudden awakening
*locked* married

## PRONUNCIATION

*Navarro* nuh-VAHR-row
*Madame* muh-DAMN
*Reina* RAY-nuh
*McGimsey* mick-JIM-zee
*Ina* EYE-nuh
*Ukiah* yoo-KAI-yuh
*Pizitz* pih-ZITZ
*Xa-wena* ha-WAY-nah

*Pomo chant (courtesy of Robert Geary):*
Oh buh-DAH-hah, ah tee-SHEESH-keeth, oh met eh-LAY-lay. Ha-WAY-nah ay-WAY-bah kay kaht-SEE-leet-bah ay-LAY-lay-deeth. Oh buh-DAH-hah, ah tee BOSH-toe seeth.

The "th" sounds at the ends of words are very lightly aspirated.

## ACKNOWLEDGEMENTS

Deep gratitude to the trees, rivers, and hills of Mendocino County, and to all the people who, voluntarily or involuntarily, served as midwives for this play: Daniel T. Denver, Nicole Ari Parker, Angela Davis, Fania Davis, Emily Morse, Mead Hunter, Leah C. Gardiner, Valerie Curtis-Newton, Ian Morgan, New Dramatists, the Helen Merrill Award committee, Marina Drummer, Robert Geary and his aunt, the last living speaker of Southeastern Pomo, Matthew Henning, Greg Tate, Adrienne Kennedy, August Wilson, and Sam Jordan. Thank you to Paula Vogel and the members of the 2007 pulitzer jury. A special thank you to all the actors who brought this play to life, particularly: Robert Beitzel, Peter Bradbury, Charlotte Colavin, Donna Duplantier, Matthew Grant, Zabryna Guevara, Adrienne Hurd, Michelle Hurd, Guiesseppe Jones, Tinashe Kajese, the late Margo Skinner, Keith Randolph Smith, Dale Soules, Ed Vassallo, and Michole Briana White.

## THORN, SPINE, AND THISTLE

**Eisa Davis**

## OH MY GIRL

**Eisa Davis**

## APPLES IN A POT

**Eisa Davis**

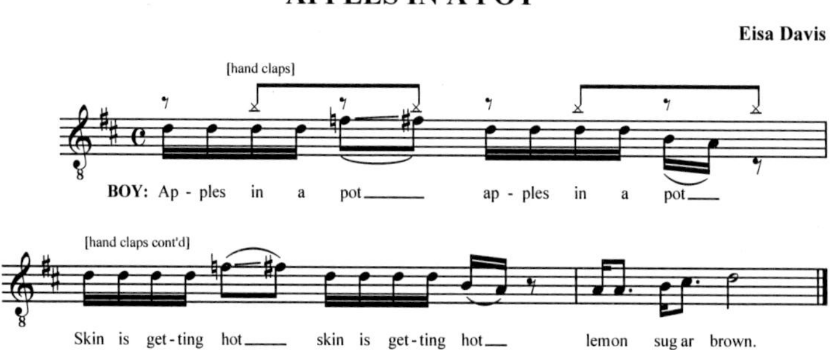

# SWEET JERK

Eisa Davis

# THE BRIEF BALLAD OF ROWAN HALE

Eisa Davis

# APPLE SHOW CALL

Anonymous Boonville
area resident

From the Reviews of
**BULRUSHER...**

"It sounds as if Eisa Davis can't help herself, she's made giddy by language...she tickles the ears of her listeners by using a regional jargon from Northern California known as Boontling...moving scenes on the banks of the pebble-strewn river...feel utterly true."
- *The New York Times*

"Race is a constant and intriguingly mutable concept in Eisa Davis' *Bulrusher*...Davis explores her themes in unexpected and evocative ways...reveals considerable thoughtfulness and originality...The still waters of *Bulrusher* turn out to run pretty deep."
- *The San Francisco Chronicle*

"At its heart, *Bulrusher* is a meditation on innocence – and an engrossing rush. When the air cleared and the lights came up at the end of Eisa Davis' gleaming marriage of poetry and myth, I was left with a sense of wonder. The play has a big heart and a wide-open soul."
- *Minneapolis-St. Paul Star Tribune*

"Mixing together issues of family, heritage, race, and love, Eisa Davis' *Bulrusher* delivers a powerful impact with a poetic, deeply realized script and story. In the hands of director Marion McClinton...the work becomes transcendent."
-TalkingBroadway.org

"*Bulrusher* brims with profound lyrical passion...a poetic play with much nuance..."
- NYTheatre.com

"Davis has powers as a writer to find beauty in almost everything, and her play pulses with compassion and life. *Bulrusher* has the kind of satisfying, uplifting ending you can only find in live theater – vibrant, poetic, immediate and thrilling."
- *Bay Area News Group*